# Ending the Violence

*A Guidebook
Based on the Experiences of
1,000 Battered Wives*

Lee H. Bowker

Revised Edition

Learning Publications, Inc.
Holmes Beach, Florida

Library of Congress Cataloging in Publication Data

Bowker, Lee Harrington
    Ending the Violence

    Bibliography: p.
    1. Wife abuse—United States.    2. Wife Abuse—
United States—Prevention    I. Title.
HV6626.B69 1986 362.8'3 85-45000
ISBN 1-55691-153-X (pbk.)

© 1998, 1986 by Lee H. Bowker

All rights reserved. No part of this book may be reproduced or transmitted in any form or by any means, electronic or mechanical, including photocopying and recording, or by any information or retrieval systems, without permission in writing from the publisher.

**Learning Publications, Inc.**
5351 Gulf Drive
P.O. Box 1338
Holmes Beach, FL 34218-1338

Consulting Editors:    Robert J. Ackerman
                          Edsel Erickson

Cover design by Karen LeMonte

Printing:  5 4 3 2 1      Year:  2 1 0 9 8

# Contents

Preface ........................................................................................... v

Acknowledgments ........................................................................ vii

1 One Thousand Violent Marriages ........................................... 1

   Jean and Jim: A Case History • Battered Wives and Their Husbands • Their Lives Together • Prior Violence • The Batterings • Two Theories that are Wrong

2 Personal Strategies ................................................................ 19

   Strategy One: Talking • Strategy Two: Promising • Strategy Three: Nonviolent Threatening • Strategy Four: Hiding • Strategy Five: Passive Defense • Strategy Six: Avoidance • Strategy Seven: Counterviolence • Effectiveness of Personal Strategies • Differences Among Women • Three Rules • A Strategy Beneath You

3 Family, Friends, and Neighbors ............................................ 34

   Family Members • Friends • Neighbors • Seeking Shelter • Comparing Informal Help – Sources • Cautions • Conclusion

4 Lawyers and Physicians ........................................................ 48

   Limitation of Medical Services • The Lawyer as Friend and Advisor • Evaluating Your Marriage

5 Law Enforcement .................................................................. 56

   Who to Call? • When the Police Arrive • Calling the District Attorney • A Comparison

6 Counseling Therapy Services ............................................... 66

   Social Service Agencies • The Clergy • Getting Your Husband to a Counselor

7 Women's Groups ................................................................... 75

   Reactions of Husbands • Finding Counseling Services • Recommendations

8 Battered Women's Shelters ................................................... 82

   Finding a Battered Women's Shelter • What Can You Expect? • Shelters are Effective • The Future of Shelters

9  What Happens to the Children?......................................................88
   The Consequences • Moving Toward Freedom • Talking
   With Your Children
10 What Works? Ending Marital Violence........................................95
   What Works Best? • Motivations • After Violence Ends •
   Battered Wives Speak Out • Why Wife Abuse?
11 Summary of Recommendations....................................................107
   Three Rules for Using Personal Strategies • Evaluating
   Your Marriage • Principles for Talking with Your Children
   • What Works Best? • Advice to Battered Women •
   Recommendations for Social Change
Appendix – For Further Reading......................................................114
   Technical Reports from the Author's Research on Battered
   Women
Index.....................................................................................................121

# Preface

*Ending the Violence* explains what battered women have done to successfully end the violence in their lives. Based on my research with one thousand battered and formerly battered women, it describes what help can be expected from family, friends, police, professionals and agencies and how to get the most support from them.

I report the results of painstaking, careful research on the histories of once-battered women who are now free of violence and women who are still being battered. Ending the Violence is written from a practical standpoint that is strongly pro-woman; giving down-to-earth advice about "what works," not rhetoric and ideology. It tells success stories, and presents an unusual view of "victims as victors." People who read this book will see how abused women have become silent heroines, and it is hoped that these examples will encourage abused women to actively seek improvements in their situations. Women do not need to tolerate violence.

The study of one thousand battered women, partly sponsored by the National Institute of Mental Health, is a technical, scientific, research report. Information was obtained through 146 in-depth interviews and formerly battered wives in southeastern Wisconsin, all of whom had become "violence-free" at least a year prior to the interview, plus 854 questionnaires sent in by women from all over the United States in response to an advertisement in Woman's Day magazine. Referring to interviews or to formerly battered women, or "our research," means that the results are drawn from the Wisconsin study. Other findings reported are taken from the entire sample of one thousand women. This sample combines the Wisconsin interviews with the questionnaires returned in the larger national study. I have illustrated most of the findings with quotes taken from "supplementary" letters the Woman's Day women contributed when they requested the questionnaires and letters they included when they returned the completed questionnaires.

In *Ending the Violence,* I eliminate complicated statistics, and describe what works in a simple, straightforward fashion. I describe different ways to reduce and prevent wife-beating, and show which strategies and help-sources are the most effective in ending the violence.

I feel uncomfortable writing about what battered women should do to save themselves and their children from their husbands' abusiveness.

To some readers, it might seem as if I am suggesting that battered wives are responsible for their own victimization. This is a dangerous untruth. Nothing justifies a man's violence against his wife. Marriage isn't slavery. Honoring and obeying are not part of the law. What a wife does for her husband and what he does for her are arrangements that must be negotiated, not demanded. In short, when a husband beats his wife, it is his fault and his fault alone. The same analysis applies to lovers who are cohabiting and to male and female homosexual relationship.

Shouldn't I have written this book for wife-beaters, not battered wives? Unfortunately, wife-beaters are not interested in the subject. So few of them want to stop their abusiveness (although a great many of them say they do) that they would never read a book about how to behave themselves. While it is true that the violence is entirely the husband's fault, the battered wife is as responsible for her behavior as he is responsible for his abusiveness. If she can do something that might influence him to stop, but holds back, she is responsible for failing to act in her own defense. This is her only responsibility in the matter, and it is this limited responsibility that I am addressing.

# Acknowledgments

I would like to express my appreciation to my staff and professional colleagues who have helped me in my wife-beating research. Special thanks are due to Kristine MacCallum, who conducted most of the 146 interviews in my first wife-beating study; to Thomas Callan, Jeffrey Koob, Michelle Arbitel and Lorie Maurer, who were responsible for data processing; and to Coleen Seagren and Donna Michalak, who produced this and other project manuscripts. Geraldine E. Rhodes, the executive editor of Woman's Day magazine, made an important contribution to the study when she agreed to print our advertisement inviting the participation of readers in an investigation of ways in which women beat wife-beating. Professors William Feyerherm, Audrey Smith, and Elam Nunnaly were generous with advice and support during my years at the University of Wisconsin-Milwaukee, as were James Breiling and Thomas Lally at the National Institute of Mental Health. Partial funding for the project was received under NIMH grant #R01MH33649. This book would not have been possible without the encouragement of Bob Ackerman and the marvelous editing skills of the staff at Learning Publications, Inc. Responsibility for the conclusions drawn in the chapters that follow is entirely my own.

Most of all, I want to thank all the brave women who participated in the study. Some of them risked further violence from their husbands and ex-husbands by agreeing to help me with this research. To the best of my knowledge, none of them ever suffered an assault as a result of their participation. Many of these women said they benefited from participating in the study. For the first time, they heard someone say that their actions to end the violence in their lives were heroic, so much so that they can now serve as role models for women who remain victims of martial violence.

## About the Author

Lee H. Bowker is the author of 17 books and scholarly monographs, including *Women and Crime in America; Women, Crime, and the Criminal Justice System; Beating Wife-Beating;* and *Masculinities and Violence.* Dr. Bowker has also published close to two hundred scientific articles, reviews and chapters in books and journals. Women's issues addressed in these publications include female drug abuse and alcoholism, female crime, women in corrections, wife-beating, rape, and the relationship between racism and sexism. Dr. Bowker is Emeritus Dean of Behavioral and Social Sciences and Professor of Sociology. He was previously Dean of the Graduate School and Research as well as Director of the Institute for Advanced Research at Indiana University of Pennsylvania, and the doctoral university of the Pennsylvania State System of Higher Education.

# 1
# One Thousand Violent Marriages

What is it like to have a violent marriage? Many readers already know. For the rest of you, this chapter will serve as an introduction to life with an assaultive partner. Wife beating is not rare in the United States, Canada, Australia, England and the rest of English-speaking western civilization. A study of family violence in the United States by Murray Straus and his associates found that one out of every six families had experienced violence between husband and wife in the previous year. Approximately a quarter of all marriages had been violent at some time in the past. Research on the sheltering of battered women carried out at the University of Regina, an analysis of police domestic crisis intervention by the Solicitor General Canada, and the publication of *Wife Battering in Canada* by the Canadian Advisory Council on the Status of Women suggests that wife-beating in Canada is as serious a problem as it is in the United States. Jocelynne Scutt has found wife-beating to be a serious problem in Australia, where it is the subject of an official report of the Australian Institute of Criminology. Some of the earliest research on battered wives was carried out in England, where the first battered women's shelter was opened. In nearby Scotland, Dobash and Dobash found evidence of an extremely serious wife-beating problem, which they published in their book, *Violence Against Wives*. These studies show that family violence is one of the most serious problems faced in western civilization.

There is no way that I can tell you all the stories of each of the thousand women in our research so I am creating a composite case history of the marriage of Jean and Jim. Their experiences are typical of the couples in the study. Their story gives you a good idea of the situations in which the women I am writing about found themselves and how most of them changed their situations, ending the violence in their lives.

## Jean and Jim: A Case History

Jean and Jim met in high school and dated off and on for several years before they became serious about their relationship. They were married in 1971. Jim never hit her while they were dating. However, there were aspects of his behavior that sometimes made Jean uneasy about him. He always wanted things his way, was jealous of her relationships with others, and seemed to have trouble controlling his temper. Jean got the impression that neither Jim nor his friends respected women, but she believed Jim when he said that she was different. Jean knew Jim's parents superficially, and they appeared to be a nice middle class family. It never occurred to her that she should closely question Jim about how his father treated his mother and whether his dad had ever beaten him when he was a child. Only after they were married did she learn that Jim had been severely disciplined until he became too big for his father to abuse, and that although Jim had never actually seen his father assault his mother, the man regularly got his way at home by threats of violence and displays of physical aggressiveness.

Their first two years of marriage were free of violence. Jim won all the arguments about anything that mattered between them. Jean felt she wasn't being treated properly and increased her resistance to Jim's domination. One night in 1973, she refused to give in and berated Jim for his behavior toward her. That was when he hit her the first time. She suffered close to 20 beatings by him during the next seven years. She was kicked, bitten, punched, and thoroughly beaten up, but Jim never used a weapon against her. She was beaten while pregnant, and their son was also beaten before the violence ended in 1980. There were also a few occasions on which Jim forced her to have sex when she didn't want it. Jim was always enraged when he beat her, and had been drinking heavily on some of the days when the beatings occurred. What set off the violence in every case was Jean's resisting Jim's will. She soon learned that if she argued back for too long, she was bound to be beaten. To minimize the violence, she avoided certain subjects and stayed out of Jim's way when he was in a bad mood. She suffered her worst battering on the day that she not only refused to give in, but also fought back physically and actually threw a coffee mug at Jim.

The battering was only part of the abuse. Jim also berated Jean about everything she did, eventually making her doubt that she was capable of doing anything right. For four years Jean sank lower and lower, too embarrassed to tell anyone about the violence. She blamed herself for Jim's behavior and didn't want anyone to know how much she had "failed in her marriage." Then, after a particularly dangerous confrontation, she took her son with her to a friend's apartment to spend the weekend. She told Irene all about her experiences of the past four years. Irene was shocked and pledged herself to help Jean to become free of the violence. Throughout their conversations during this and two subsequent visits, as well as many phone conversations and daytime visits while Jim was at work, Irene emphasized Jean's rights as a human being and what a good person Jean was. She had confidence in Jean, and it started to rub off.

Jean puzzled over the problem of Jim's violence. She didn't want to destroy him and their family. She wanted him to stop beating her and to begin treating her like an equal in family decisions. With Irene's help, Jean decided to seek the assistance of a professional counselor to help her plan her future. Jean didn't want to involve the police in her marriage because that would bring the violence into the public eye, possibly hurting Jim's chances for a promotion at the office.

Jean's counselor was a social worker who didn't know anything about family violence that she hadn't learned from her clients. Nevertheless, she helped Jean become stronger, continuing the process that began in Jean's talks with Irene. As they discussed how to deal with Jim, it became clear that it would take a major shock to jolt him out of the cycle of violence. Jean finally decided to hire a lawyer and to pretend to file for a divorce, intending to drop the action later after Jim agreed to see a counselor. It was easier for Jean to hire a lawyer than it is for many battered women because Jim had not taken away all her money (a common way that batterers keep their wives under their thumbs). Her social worker recommended a lawyer who specialized in divorces, though not in marital violence.

The lawyer sent Jim an official notification of Jean's intention to file for a divorce. He was furious and demanded that she drop the legal action, but Jean thought the strategy was working because Jim didn't hit her when he threw his fit. In the following weeks, Jean and Jim had endless discussions about their marriage and the violence. Jim agreed never to beat her again, provided that Jean didn't push him too far, but he refused to see a counselor or join a men's group for batterers. Jean wasn't satisfied with this, so she put the divorce on hold instead of dropping it. She knew that Jim was no longer in control of her life.

As the weeks stretched into months, Jim kept his promise to avoid battering Jean. He even allowed her to have her way on several minor issues, such as which movie they would go to on a Saturday evening. Jean had thought violence was the only major problem in her marriage. Now she realized that Jim's disregard of her needs and rights had chipped away at her love for him over the years. She still wanted to be married, particularly for the sake of her son, but she no longer wished to share her life with Jim.

Jean and her son left Jim forever in early 1981 as she reactivated the divorce action. Realizing that he had lost everything, Jim pleaded with Jean to return, offering to enter therapy or to do anything else she wanted if she would just return and cook his meals. While Jean pitied him, she knew she never would go back. Jim's continual dominating and uncompromising behavior, more than the violence itself, had destroyed their relationship. Having to face this was part of what had made Jean strong. Now she was strong enough to face life without a husband and to simultaneously hold down a full-time job and raise her son without help. She wasn't sure whether she wanted to remarry, but she knew if she did, it would have to be a relationship between equals, one with a man who respected women and had no history of violence.

## Battered Wives and Their Husbands

Jean is typical of the 1,000 women who participated in our research. Nearly all of the couples were legally married during the time when the violence occurred. Both husband and wife were raised in working class or middle class homes. The average woman was 38 years old. Half of the battered wives were Protestant, a third Catholic. More than nine out of every ten women were white. Half of them attended church once a month or more and a similar proportion had completed at least one college course. One out of every nine women had received a four-year college degree.

The husbands were an average of three years older than their wives. Six out of every seven husbands were white. They were less likely than their wives to be church members, to have attended church regularly, or to have gone to college. However, they were more likely to be college graduates than their wives. Half of these men had served in the armed forces, with an average length of service of three years; one in three had seen combat overseas. Slightly less than half of them had participated in a major violent sport such as football or ice hockey.

## Their Lives Together

Most of the couples had one or two children, and a small number of families included children that one of the parents brought with them from a previous marriage. The average couple moved three times during their relationship. More than sixty percent of the couples had purchased one or more homes during their years together. The wives had held at least one job outside of the home in nearly three-quarters of the marriages. From the outside, these appeared to be normal, stable, productive American families.

In a typical marriage, the couple had been married ten years after dating for more than a year. Approximately half of the wives were dissatisfied with their marriages apart from the batterings, and there was a tendency for dissatisfaction to increase over time in many of the marriages. Approximately two-thirds of the women were dissatisfied with their marriages in each of several areas: communication with their husbands, affection, sexual behavior, the amount of time spent together, and the quality of their participation in joint activities. The couples continuously disagreed on half-a-dozen issues throughout their marriages, and suffered intense marital stress because of these disagreements. Common areas of disagreement were finances, the batterings, chores, children, drinking or drugs, and time spent together. The husbands dominated these marriages, the wives winning less than one argument out of every 30 during their first year together and one of every eight in their most recent year together. Over three-quarters of the couples separated at least once. In several marriages, there were more than a half-dozen separations. These usually consisted of the wife's taking shelter away from her husband to avoid his violent attacks.

## Prior Violence

Most of the parents of the battered women we studied were not violent. Three-quarters of the women never had witnessed violence between their parents during their childhoods, and less than half had ever been hit by their parents. Considering the violence which was to come for them, it is surprising how few of these women had been beaten before they met their future mates.

Husbands were exposed to a higher level of childhood violence than their wives. More than half of them observed violence between their parents, sometimes frequently. Approximately six of every ten husbands were assaulted by their parents, and the assaults occurred frequently in most of these violent families. These are doubtless underestimates, for there must have been many violent incidents that the husbands never described to their wives.

In most of the battering relationships, the wives had little warning of their impending victimization while dating. Premarital violence occurred in only one relationship out of every four. It was usually limited to slapping and other minor forms of violence, making it easy for the wives to assume that it would not occur again.

Jealousy was the most common theme in the incidents of premarital violence. More than a few of the men thought of their future wives as personal property, and became enraged whenever the women showed any independence, particularly by paying attention to other men. There were a few cases in which the suitors so thoroughly dominated their future wives through violence and threats that the women believed they had to complete their marriage plans in order to avoid severe violence and retaliation. These women had no idea how to deal successfully with the unexpected eruption of premarital violence, and rarely sought help.

In some of the relationships where premarital violence did

not occur, the woman was warned of her future husband's violence when he threw temper tantrums that stopped short of overt violence. These tantrums reinforced the men's domination of their fiancées. It is possible that some of these temper outbursts would have proceeded to violence if the women hadn't given in. Some of the women reacted to the displays of temper by suppressing their natural reactions, thus avoiding inciting their mates to more extreme behavior. The temper outbursts, like the premarital violence, were invariably followed by profuse apologies, which often convinced a woman that her husband would soon straighten out. In every case, the women were wrong in tolerating their husbands' poor behavior, for all of them were about to become battered wives.

## The Batterings

The average woman in our study suffered her first battering two years after marrying. Many details about this first incident were recalled by the women interviewed. The husband had been drinking all evening, although he was still in control of his behavior. His violence against her was limited to several slaps and a kick. Marital rape, child abuse, and extensive beatings were rare in the first incident, but they became more common as one violent incident followed another. Most women had been beaten at least 20 times before the violence came to an end, many of them on more than 200 occasions. More than half of them saw their children assaulted by their husbands (70% of those who had children with the batterers), and just under half were beaten while pregnant. Seventy-two of the women suffered miscarriages from the beatings. The majority of the women were raped by their husbands, most of them numerous times. In addition to being hit, slapped, kicked, punched, bitten, and generally beaten up, many of the women were threatened or assaulted with dangerous weapons. Cold statistics cannot communicate the tragedies that women suffer. Consider, for example, these quotations from the women in our research:

> I have had clothes ripped off me and torn into shreds. I have had both eyes blackened on several occasions and my eardrum was fractured as a result of repeated slapping.

> As I was driving home [my husband] was on the passenger side and we got into a minor argument. He began punching me *very* hard. I was all over the highway. He made me pull over and move to the passenger side and I did. Driving, he then started on the other arm and spat on me...

> [My husband] wrestled me in the kitchen, put his foot on my neck and proceeded to pull my finger backwards. The bone snapped...

> I had just gotten out of the hospital about two weeks ago. [My husband] was leaving for a two-month Army stint and he got mad because his uniforms weren't packed or ironed right. That time I got stamped and kicked into unconsciousness...

> He hit me across the face with his fist and snarled, "Come on, fight like a man." The blow knocked me to the floor, he grabbed me by the hair and yanked me to a somewhat standing position. "I'll show you," he sneered. He started choking me to the point that I could no longer stand, my knees buckled and I fell to the floor with his hands still around my neck.

> Three weeks after we were married, I was hit for stepping on a combat boot my husband just shined...

The reason for my being manhandled, shoved, slammed, nearly murdered twice, spit on, sworn at is FEAR. [My husband] nearly strangled me when I said he had been cruel to me...

[As a result of the beatings], my cheek is wired in two places, my jaw was broken, and I have a silicone implant to hold my eye up, because the bone was completely shattered.

He has never beaten me to the point where I need medical care, rather he limits it to black and blue arms, bloody ears from pulling them so hard while he screams at me, welts on my back from hard slaps and never-ending verbal abuse...

[My husband] started shoving me as we left the party and contined through the hotel lobby. When we reached the parking lot he began throwing me against cars and then to the ground. Two unknown young men saw it and asked him to stop. He continued. They jumped him and beat him up requiring plastic surgery on his face. His only comment was that "two wimps" did this to him. My torn clothing, cuts and bruises were nothing to him...

[My husband] was an attorney and counselor who eventually went into divorce law. He would take pictures of clients [who had been beaten] and show me [saying] if I didn't be careful it would be worse [for me] than this or that woman was. One night he came home and started shooting [at me]. After he had fired four shots and grazed my shoulder, I finally got him to stop.

I was put down on a bed with [my husband] lying on top of me holding my hands and feet, he took a pen and wrote on my neck and breast and tried to twist my breasts off.

The worse part came on Christmas Eve. My present was a bad beating. [My husband] wrapped a vacuum cleaner cord around my neck and almost did me in...

...My head ached with pain, from both the direct fist blows to my head and from being yanked from the floor by my hair everytime he knocked me down. Blood formed around my right eye. My jaws were already starting to swell and the choke marks on my neck didn't hurt nearly as bad as the inside of my throat. He had previously made the comment, "I can hurt you real bad and never leave a mark on your body..."

The violence continued for years for many of the women, even when they were pregnant.

My husband knocked out [my] tooth, punched me in the abdomen when I was pregnant, pushed me against plastic shower doors and cracked a rib.

It took me eight years and the death of an unborn daughter to make me more angry at him than scared of him. There were four children in that time and two dead babies, both caused by him. I was three months pregnant and got slapped, kicked, and punched. I was thrown on the bed and had hair torn out and [he] attempted strangulation — luckily the cops arrived then...

[My husband] beat me so bad I lost a child. He put me in the hospital for a week.

The children were likely to be beaten too, sometimes as severely as the mother.

[My husband] was drunk and ended up hitting my daughter in the head with a cast aluminum skillet...

My four year-old daughter is an abused child. She screams at night in her sleep and has nightmares as a result...

I have lived with this for 30 years now. [Even] my grandson is a victim of abuse. It has left him blind. And to think I stayed for the sake of the children.

I experienced the fear, anxiety, and horror of being abused and helplessly watched the abuse of my children.

My husband is also a child abuser. My 14 year-old son has been beaten since he was a toddler.

Domination through violence invariably means domination in sexual matters.

After calling me names, [my husband] then expected me to "jump in the sack" and "relieve his sexual anxieties" as he phrased it. I have four children, and one miscarriage and one abortion as a result of his need to relieve sexual anxieties two and three times a day. He told me he owned me and my body...

[My husband] didn't really force me physically. He

just made me feel so rotten and guilty for not wanting sex that I felt like I had to. Most of the time it was like that because he'd keep bugging me to give him oral sex and it turned me off.

When [my husband] wanted to assert himself and feel like a man, he would twist my nipples or goose me suddenly and painfully.

Sexual domination becomes marital rape when violence and threats of violence enter the picture.

I truly do not know what a "satisfying sexual realtionship" is. I was subjected to repeated, violent, rape-like sessions over a long period of time...

Not only was I beaten but raped by my husband. There are people that say a husband cannot rape his wife — because it is his wife — but I disagree 100%.

My husband was very possessive of me yet he forced me to have sex with another man so he could watch.

Alot of [my husband's] abuse was sexual. He'd often tie me to our bed. Once or twice he decided he'd like three women at a time. When I awoke with two other women in bed with us, it about sent me out of my head...

For some men, the "need" for sexual dominance extends as far as their own children.

I was in a violent marriage and my daughters were sexually abused by their father.

[My husband] attacked my 13 year-old daughter sexually while I was at work and told her he'd beat her if she told...

My husband faced eight counts of incest with our *only* daughter...

Perhaps these stories will help us to grasp the severe tragedy of wife-beating and also see it in its variety. No two families are identical, and male domination and violence develops different nuances in each family setting. However, there are theories which attempt to explain spouse abuse: two are definitely wrong but widely believed. For this reason they bear discussion. Then more plausible explanations will be considered.

## Two Theories That Are Wrong

We often hear that battered women have tended to suffer much violence from their parents, so they "invite" the beatings they receive from their husbands. This is wrong! We also hear that batterers are likely to be alcoholics or mentally ill. This is also wrong! The presumption is that batterers would not beat their wives and children if they were healthy. Our research provides little evidence to support the first theory and no evidence at all to support the second.

The idea that some women are victimization-prone, inviting mistreatment through their passivity and acceptance of beatings, amounts to no more than blaming the victim. In victim-blaming theories, the victims are somehow made responsible for their own victimization. For example, victim-blaming explains that minority groups fail to achieve equality because of their own bad habits or inherent limitations instead of emphasizing the effects of discrimination. Battered women probably were not much more likely than non-battered women to have witnessed violence between their parents or to have been beaten by their parents. The women we interviewed rarely, if ever, were violently victimized by anyone else. In short, they were not victimization-prone.

Not so for their violent spouses. Their husbands were exposed to an unusually high level of violence starting in early childhood. Many of them were brutalized by their fathers, or became involved in violent situations with friends, acquaintances and strangers. Our research, like other recent research on wife-beating, shows that it is the violent background of the husbands rather than the victimization history of the wives that should be part of any theory of family violence. Even if battered wives could be shown to be victimization-prone, it wouldn't justify their continued battering. Wife-beating is a serious assaultive crime, a felony which is punishable with prison terms of as long as twenty years.

Are wives beaten mainly because their husbands drink too much, or have emotional problems? I think not! There are some cases where this is true, just as it is always possible to find a few examples to "prove" any theory, but I believe that these factors are not major causes of wife-beating. There is no evidence that most wife-beaters are any more mentally ill than you and I are. Some drink to excess and others do not. Despite their heavy drinking, the men with alcohol problems do not seem to be completely out of control when they beat their wives. They carefully lock the doors, or behave in a gentlemanly fashion until they get home from a party, or wait until the children are asleep to assault their spouses. Most men who beat their wives when drunk also batter them when sober. Drinking releases inhibitions, but since the husbands are well aware of this fact, they may choose to drink to excuse their violence or at least beg off from taking responsibility for their violent behavior by referring to their drinking problem.

If violent husbands do not beat their wives because of drinking or other personality problems, how can we explain wife-beating? *The key to understanding wife-beating is the struggle for power and domination.* Abusive husbands use violence to keep their wives obedient, terrified, and sometimes in virtual slavery. In its mildest form, wife-beating allows husbands to be sure that family decisions will be made the way they want them. These men believe that men must dominate their wives because it is the natural order of things, because women are morally weak, or for some other equally demeaning reason. They may also believe that they work harder than their wives, so they deserve their way at home; or that their needs are more insistent because of their nature as men. Beliefs such as these, as well as the expectation that a "real man" must dominate his wife, are often reinforced by the batterers' male friends at bars, sporting events, on the job and in other settings that are male-dominated, as well as by pornography and many other publications, television programs, and movies. Here are some examples presented to us of the domination suffered by women:

> My husband not only convinced *me* that I was "ugly, useless, underdeveloped, and not fit to be called a human being" but he managed to convince two of our three children the same.

> The sad part of it all was he enjoyed the power his meanness gave to him. When I didn't work, I was lazy. When I did, I was only working to meet other men. I could not talk to people who were old friends, or he would embarrass them by being abusive verbally. He would ask friends of my father "how often they slept with me". I gradually cut all people out of my life, and it did not matter; he accused me of sleeping with my psychiatrist and any other service persons I encountered.

I was rapidly coming to believe that I deserved the beatings and verbal abuse, that I was the "nothing" he termed me.

I was married at 15 years old. I was not pregnant. (He was 22 years old.) I was not allowed to speak in a loud voice or talk back if he hadn't asked me a question. If I didn't answer quickly, he would usually slap me...

I would stress that a wife beater does more than beat [his wife]. He makes fun of her, refuses to give her money, embarrasses her in front of [others] and says everyone else is out-of-step, not him.

I continually have to tolerate his criticism of most everything I do.

When I took out my own checking account, [my husband] stopped all financial contributions to the household.

I have allowed myself to become a virtual prisoner for the past four years.

[My husband] has told our daughters that I don't care for them as well as him. He told them I had an affair with my brother-in-law which is a lie. He tells them I don't do anything around the house, and I am the one who's ruined our home life and who's responsible for his getting hurt. [But] I can't seem to leave. He says the girls would never go with me. He won't let them because I don't deserve to have them let alone deserve to live.

[In my experience] the husband usually attempts to

isolate his victim (or at least *convince* her she is isolated) by preventing individual friendships to strengthen so that she can trust a neighbor or co-worker to help her.

I always thought it was my fault. If only I was better or prettier, or had black hair instead of red. I was too afraid to leave; finally I got too afraid to stay.

Instead of being mentally ill, *most wife-beaters are no more than extreme examples of the sexist values, beliefs and standards that permeate western civilization.* Batterers are not so much mentally ill as they are overconformists to the macho culture of male domination and sexism that has only recently begun to change. Violence will not disappear from their marriages so long as they persist in their views of male dominance and female inferiority. The problem of their violence cannot be solved apart from the problem of unbalanced marital power in their families. Teaching batterers to control their tempers, helping them realize why they hated their mothers, and other counseling approaches that ignore the question of marital power are unlikely to substantially reduce marital violence.

#  2
# Personal Strategies

There are seven common strategies that women use to try to get their husbands to stop beating them. These are: (1) trying to talk their husbands out of further beatings; (2) extracting promises to end the abuse; (3) threatening some sort of nonviolent action, such as contacting the police or filing for a divorce; (4) hiding or escaping during the beatings; (5) using passive defenses to protect themselves as much as possible from serious injury; (6) avoiding their husbands during periods of high potential for violence; and (7) fighting back. Avoidance is a preventive strategy used prior to the onset of a violent episode; hiding, passive defense and counterviolence are used while the violence is in progress; and talking, promising and nonviolent threatening are employed between batterings.

While I discuss each of these seven personal strategies one by one, please note that battered wives usually use two or more strategies at a time, trying different combinations until they either find one that is effective or they are forced to add the resources of formal or informal help-sources to their personal efforts. It is also true that the personal strategies overlap, so that it is not always easy to know where one strategy begins and another ends.

## Strategy One: Talking

Talking husbands out of further beatings consists mainly of rational arguments about why violence is wrong and how bad it is for the marriage. Those who use this strategy try to lead the husband into seeing the error of his ways, and to stimulate guilt over his abusiveness. Nearly three-quarters of the battered wives we studied attempted to talk their husbands out of further violence. When talking didn't work (and it didn't help at all for most women), the wife usually gave up trying to talk sensibly with her husband about his abusiveness.

For some couples, talking is just a brief discussion, while for others, it is a continuous dialogue spread over many years. It is impossible to discuss the problem with some husbands because they become irrational whenever wife beatings are discussed. Other men insist on blaming alcohol for their violence or pretend that their wives are really in control of the marriage. Another ploy used by batterers is to say that they will be happy to end the abuse if their wives concede all independence and obey them without question. A woman who agrees to this trades much of her freedom for her husband's good behavior. Even worse, she sets up a situation in which any display of her own anger is interpreted as giving him the right to assault her. Some of the women we surveyed used talking in the following ways.

> For the first time in our life together, we sat down and talked through our problems. [My husband] agreed he needed to learn to control his anger and talk instead of yelling threats. He called a local helpline right there for an appointment to see a counselor.

> I finally spoke up [to my husband] and said, "You're not my boss! You're supposed to be my husband. I'm a married woman and I'm my own boss." I got it that time, but I hit him back...

> [My husband] said he was going to kill me and then himself. That was scary but we talked and he changed his mind.

## Suggestions

If you try the talking strategy, keep calm and rational. Try not to show fear no matter how afraid you are. Finally, embarrass him by displaying your injuries (for example, don't wear slacks and long sleeves to hide your bruises) and confront him with the results of his abusiveness in any other way you can. However, talking may make your husband so angry that he increases his violence against you. If this occurs, it is best to drop the strategy of talking and move on to other strategies.

## Strategy Two: Promising

It is only a short step from talking about the battering to trying to obtain the batterer's promise to end the violence. Promising goes beyond talking in that the abuser makes a verbal commitment never to beat his wife again. Sounds good, doesn't it? Don't be fooled. Promising occurred as often as just plain talking in the women's marriages, but it was even less successful. Only one out of every eight women whose husbands promised to end the violence found that promises made any difference at all.

> I went away for four months, I started a divorce. My husband promised to quit drinking if I'd come back. He quit for seven years...he started again.

> [My husband] keeps telling me he's sorry and I'm the only woman he wants and loves and he won't drink anymore. I feel sorry for him and stick it out, hoping he will change like he says he will.

> I want to get a divorce, but he keeps trying to get me back with promises and crying...
>
> I have been living on and off in a personal hell for ten years, [during which] his begging and apologies always worked.
>
> [The problem] isn't solved. [My husband] agreed to some conditions which I said must be met, then when we were back together, he didn't keep any of them.

The arguments leading to promises to end the violence in the couples were sometimes based on love or morality, but the husband usually made the promise "spontaneously" in the context of a general discussion or argument about the abuse. A husband who spontaneously promised to end the abuse was more likely to take his promise seriously than one who felt compelled to make such a promise.

## Suggestions

Don't be encouraged by a man who apologizes and cries after each incident, promising never to abuse you again. He usually forgets his promise the next time he becomes enraged at you. Another pattern to watch for is the man who apologizes and makes promises when sober, and then returns to the abuse when he drinks heavily. Many of the women who were initially convinced that their husbands were sincere when making these promises eventually learned to ignore them and to realize that the promises were just a part of a cycle of violence designed to dominate them.

## Strategy Three: Nonviolent Threatening

Nonviolent threatening, with no weapon, consists mainly of threats to call the police, press charges, leave home, get a divorce, or do something else to expose the batterer before the community. Threats to tell the husband's relatives or friends were rarely made by the women, perhaps because they realized their uselessness as deterrents to further abuse. Slightly more than three-quarters of the women in my research used nonviolent threatening at least once, and one out of every three who tried it found it helpful in reducing or ending the violence.

> I finally got up enough nerve to ask my husband for a divorce and he cried, begged and promised [he'd] reform.

> I *lied* to [my husband], told him I'd filled out all the necessary papers; and if he ever struck me again, I'd sign them...Once, after a beating, I'd [even] lied that I'd gone to a doctor who had photos of my bruises. I told him this proof would go on file.

> My arms were bruised from shoulder to wrist. I had slides taken and threatened [my husband] with them.....the violence did cease for awhile.

> I told [my husband] straight out that he either get help now or get lost. The emotional and financial losses are too great to go on...

> When I threatened to file charges [against my husband], he punished me in a new way — repeated affairs.

### Suggestions

The only way to be successful with the threatening strategy is to convince your husband that the threats are serious, not frivolous. He must believe that you will follow through on the threat if he does not end his abuse. For this reason, the successful use of threatening was often combined with the involvement of a formal help-source. For example, some women made arrangements with an attorney for divorce proceedings to begin, so that their threat to begin the divorce was a very immediate one. Other women called the police, or involved the district attorney in order to make their threats seem realistic. Threatening sometimes worked because the husbands agreed to enter treatment for their abusive behavior. Had they not gone to a counselor or joined a therapy group, they might never have stopped beating their wives. The women studied provided many examples of nonviolent threatening.

## Strategy Four: Hiding

Hiding, which also includes escape, consists of techniques such as running out of the house, hiding in another room, and hiding behind furniture. Women sometimes run out in the yard or lock themselves in the bedroom to avoid further battering. They hide in bathrooms, cellars, closets, and in any other place that has a lock on the door. Hiding was used about as often as promising and threatening by the battered wives. Hiding sometimes prevented further injuries, yet it also resulted in increased violence in nearly a quarter of the cases. Men who like to dominate and crush their wives don't want them running away for even an hour. They want to control them during every minute of their lives.

> I usually could tell by the look in his eyes when [my husband] got mad and I'd better get out of his way or try to run.
>
> When [my husband] goes into one of his rages and

tries to kill me I run for my life and just get out the door in time.

When [my husband] starts his "uproar" game, I sneak out of the house. He has usually cooled down by the time I return; [but] I must sneak because if he knows I am leaving the scene and spoiling his rage, I am detained at all costs.

I had learned from previous occasions to get away from [my husband] when he was in this [raucous] mood.

**Suggestions**

Hiding is successful when it removes you from the batterer. If you spend days living in your bathroom, attic or cellar, or nights in the backyard, you are seriously disrupting your life. That is a high price to pay to maintain your marriage. Besides, there is the danger that your husband may beat you even worse, perhaps after he has broken down a door to reach you or locked the front door or ripped up your clothing to keep you from leaving the house and running down the street. Some of the battered women who left their houses had nowhere to go, and thus felt compelled to eventually return. Unfortunately, violent husbands who control all of the family's resources leave their wives with few choices for escaping and hiding from the batterings.

## Strategy Five: Passive Defense

An instinctive and passive reaction when suffering a beating is to try to cover one's body with hands, arms, and feet. Despite being a commonly used strategy, this passive defense almost never has a positive impact on men's behavior. In fact, passive defense makes some men more angry, in which case they may intensify their abuse. Almost all battered women studied used passive defense at one time or another, but unfortunately it only led to increased violence by their mates.

> I raised my arms to protect my breasts and face. He kicked me in the legs, thighs, the back saying, "Come on, get up and fight like a man, I'll show you!" I prayed, "Dear God, please let me get away."

**Suggestions**

When you protect the body with hands, arms, and legs, you are probably crying or otherwise showing your submission to your husband's dominance. A few husbands may be moved to end the violence by the crying, which makes them realize how much they are hurting their wives. Also, there are those husbands who are reassured that they are in control, so they don't need to continue to beat their wives further. On the other hand, sadistic husbands will be stimulated by the crying to prolong the beatings. The harder their wives cry, the more their husbands beat them. Some degree of passive defense is instinctive. However, passive defense is not a good strategy to use in your efforts to become free of the violence.

## Stragegy Six: Avoidance

Unlike the other personal strategies, avoidance is a preventive effort used before the violence begins. The battered women often attempted to avoid an assault by keeping out of their husbands' sight or by refusing to engage in an argument (biting the tongue, so to speak) begun by their husbands. In some cases, the women would leave home before their husbands arrived from work when they thought a battering was coming. Like hiding, avoidance meant that these women had to surrender part of their freedom for a chance of decreasing their husbands' violence. Even when avoidance was successful in reducing the violence (which it was for close to half the women studied), it was at the expense of losing more ground in the fight to live a normal life and have a marriage of equals instead of a dictatorship. Consider the following personal statements:

> I just won't argue with him and then he won't hit me. I don't want to put the kids through this [either]...

> [I have] to try to leave the house when even the slightest hint of temper shows [in my husband].

> A friend knew he had beaten me before so I took [my husband's] advice and left and stayed at my girlfriend's house...

The batterers gave indications that they were working up to a violent incident. Some drank heavily and others slammed doors. Just being in a bad mood was a sure indication that a few of the violent husbands would shortly find an excuse to start a fight. Many wives also learned that there were things they did not dare to do around their husbands if they wanted to avoid a beating. Forbidden behaviors included talking with other men, showing anger toward their husbands, bringing up sensitive subjects and disputing their husbands' opinions and decisions.

## Suggestions

Do not count on avoidance to solve your problems. Avoidance is a way of living with your husband's violence, not ending it. Using avoidance is at best a delaying tactic while you marshall more potent forces to end the violence.

## Strategy Seven: Counterviolence

The counterviolence used most often by the battered women consisted of kicking, biting and punching. Other techniques included slapping and hitting back with or throwing a hard object. Two-thirds of the women fought back physically at least once. Unfortunately again, this proved to be dangerous in that it was more likely to incense the batterers, stimulating far worse beatings, than to lead to the termination of the violence and an apology.

Counterviolence isn't usually planned. Women who fight back with a weapon grab anything that is handy when they are being attacked, including furniture, kitchen utensils, and telephones. Knives and poison were rarely used. However, in a few cases they had a significant effect in ending or decreasing the violence. Threats of violence, when they did work, were most likely to be effective when the husbands were convinced that their wives were serious. For example, more than one woman pointed out to her husband that she could kill him when he was sleeping if he continued to beat her. On the rare occasions when such counterviolence worked, it was usually because the husbands were genuinely afraid of the homicidal threats made by their wives; the threats shocked them into realizing the seriousness of their own behavior, or they came to "respect" their wives more for having fought back. Gaining your husband's respect by engaging in behavior that is valued in the world of macho men lowers you to his moral level instead of raising him to your moral level.

Some of the counterviolence strategies used by the battered women were extremely dangerous. Others, luckily, were successful. Several of their stories follow, beginning with threats of violence and progressing to assaults.

> I never forgave [my husband] and I never will; and my threat to kill him if it happens again, still stands.

I believe the only reason he has not hit me in this past year is because I warned him last time not to fall asleep if he did.

The time he spanked the children with a strap and hit our eleven year-old son with a board, I threatened him with a rifle.

His mother will say, "I am tired of seeing my son beaten to a bloody pulp." That happened one time when I hit back with a telephone when he had me on the floor choking me in a drunken rage.

[My husband] nearly beat me to death. I picked up a hammer in self defense and chased him out of the house. I lost two teeth, sight in my right eye, had a broken arm and three broken ribs. [But] I ended up in jail for assault with a deadly weapon...

[My husband] brought me to his level at times. I'd break a glass or throw things I never dared before.

I did at times hit him first and strike back in self defense, but it only made matters worse.

The first time [my husband] slapped my face, I was thoroughly shocked. I responded by digging my nails into his arms and scratching the length of his arms. I remember being slapped and then my whole body went numb. When I came to, I was standing with a broom in my hand. I shouted, "You son-of-a-b_____h. Don't you ever hit me again." And with that I hit him in the ribs with the broom. It knocked the wind out of him and he fell on the floor.

## Suggestions

When you read a story about the successful use of counterviolence, it sounds great. That might tempt you to use it yourself. Please don't! Of the 690 battered women studied who reported on the effectiveness of counterviolence, only 8 percent found it to be very effective and an additional 10 percent rated it as somewhat effective. For more than eight out of ten women, counterviolence did not work. What's worse, 58 percent of the women suffered even more violence as their punishment for physically challenging their husbands. If you have children, the dangers of using counterviolence are even greater. They may be pulled into the situation and hurt. Even if they aren't they will see their mother lowering herself to the same animal level as their father.

Counterviolence is the most dangerous strategy and it is one of the least successful. It is twice as dangerous as nonviolent threatening, three times as dangerous as passive defense or talking, six times as dangerous as avoidance, and nearly ten times as dangerous as getting your husband to promise to end the batterings. I wouldn't bet against odds like that. You shouldn't either.

## Effectiveness of Personal Strategies

There are two different ways of evaluating the effectiveness of these strategies. One is to consider their immediate effect on the husband's behavior. The other is to judge their contribution to permanently ending the violence. The strategies that were somewhat effective in the short run were promising and threatening. These had positive effects on the batterers slightly more than half the time. (Either the batterers apologized and became more agreeable for the time being, or they left their wives alone for a while without admitting having been wrong for beating them.) Talking and avoidance only worked well in a third of the cases, counterviolence in a quarter of the cases, hiding rarely, and passive defense almost never.

Comparing short and long-term effects shows that although promises to end the battering may seem believable at the time they are made, they do not hold up. When next they become enraged at their wives, violent husbands are quick to forget their promises and apologies. On the other hand, nonviolent threatening, hiding, counterviolence and avoidance become increasingly effective as the couple becomes less intimate over the years. Wives who consistently practice these strategies are around their husbands as little as possible, so they slowly grow apart. Nonviolent threatening and counterviolence take the opposite tack. The wives who use these strategies directly confront their husbands and fight it out, either verbally or physically, and many of them suffer more beatings as a result of their courageous behavior.

## Differences Among Women

The seven personal strategies seemed to work or not work as well for one woman as for another, regardless of age, occupation, or income. Also, the personal characteristics of the husbands seemed to have little effect on the success of these strategies. It did not matter whether either spouse had been beaten by their parents or had seen their father beat their mothers. If some personal strategies for ending the battering work better with one kind of family than another, it is not apparent in our research.

However, there was a consistency of effectiveness from one battering incident to another. A strategy that worked well in one battering incident was also likely to be successful in other battering incidents. When a battered woman discovered a strategy or a combination of strategies that worked for her, she was then able to repeat it each time her husband abused her.

When any or all of these strategies were effective, the violence occurred less often and when it did occur, it was less severe than it was in marriages where the personal strategies did not work at all. In addition, families in which one or more of these strategies worked were less dominated by the husbands than the other violent families. In other words, these personal strategies are unlikely to work unless your husband agrees to let you have more of a say in decisions that affect yourself and your family.

## Three Rules

There are three rules that battered women should follow when they use personal strategies to combat the violence:

1. *The first one is that nothing works unless you convince your husband that you are dead serious about ending the batterings.* You must be consistent in your opposition to his violent behavior. You can never allow him or anyone else to convince you that you deserve to be beaten. Your husband is entitled to protect himself if you hit him first. Otherwise, there is nothing you could possibly have done that would justify violence against you — not being bad tempered, not keeping a sloppy house, not standing up for your rights, not refusing to have sex whenever he wants, and not failing to cook meals the way he wants them. If your husband hits you, he is totally wrong. There may be many reasons for his violence, but there is no excuse for it.

2. *The second rule is that verbal strategies based on caring are not worth trying unless your husband cares a great deal about you.* If your marriage isn't that strong, and if your husband cares more about dominating you than about your welfare, you are better off avoiding him and threatening to divorce him or have him arrested. When negative pressure is the only way to keep your husband from assaulting you, you should seriously consider why you still want to stay with him. Violence and the failure of strategies such as talking and promising are often indications that your husband does not care about you as much as you

thought he did. That casts a different light on the future of your marriage.

3. *The final rule is that you must not allow a pattern of violence to develop in your marriage.* The more deeply ingrained a violent pattern becomes, the more it becomes a fundamental part of your married life. In view of the success achieved by women with nonviolent threatening, you should use this strategy at the beginning of the violence instead of years later. Even better, make it absolutely clear to your husband when you marry him that you will never tolerate even a single assault. Make him believe that the first time he hits you, you will leave him immediately. When he believes you, your likelihood of having a violence-free marriage will be greatly improved.

## A Strategy Beneath You

There is one personal strategy that I haven't mentioned. It is to obey your husband in all things, anticipating his every wish while denying yourself even the slightest chance of living a normal life.

> The only way to stop my husband is to be totally dependent on him. He likes this.

Total surrender of self isn't seriously examined as a strategy because no marriage is worth the complete destruction of yourself as a person. If this is the only way to avoid being beaten, it is time to pack your bags. Begin planning to leave as soon as possible. Call a women's crisis line, women's group, or battered women's shelter for advice, and contact trusted relatives (your relatives, not his) and friends for help. A week by himself may shock your husband into a new frame of mind. In the meantime, you can do some hard thinking whether the relationship is worth continuing, even if the violence ceases.

# 3
# Family, Friends and Neighbors

Nothing is more natural than to turn to a friend or family member for help with a personal problem, and yet many battered wives never share their secret with any of the people who care about them. There are many reasons for this. It is embarrassing to describe the beatings to others, particularly if you mistakenly believe it is your own fault. Some women feel the existence of violence in their marriages means they don't have good marriages, so they want to keep it to themselves. Others don't want to ruin their husband's image with their friends. More important than any of these reasons, many husbands demand total secrecy, promising terrible beatings or even murder if their wives ever tell the truth about what goes on in their marriages.

Isolation is an enemy of violence-free marriages. If you keep your husband's behavior secret, you are playing right into his hands. He can then do anything he wants to you, and nobody will be able to put social pressure on him to be more reasonable. Family, friends and neighbors can do many things to help you, as we will see later in this chapter. You are not alone! Help is available for the asking.

There are two ways to judge whether someone is an appropriate person to approach for help. First they must strongly disapprove of wife-beating. If they think that men might under any conditions need to beat their wives to keep them in line, forget them. The second point is that they must care enough about you as a person to be courageous. Helping battered wives is dangerous, as I found out myself when an enraged husband smashed the windshield of our family car with a beer bottle. Anyone who helps you risks the possibility that your husband will find out about them and insult, harass, or assault them. You probably have a number of friends, relatives and neighbors who disapprove of wife-beating and who care enough about you to risk helping you. Start with the best one, and then involve others too.

The more people who become involved with your problem, the sooner you will be free of violence. They can increase the social pressure on your husband to end the abusiveness. They can encourage you to take control of your life and can help you see all your strong points, (your husband will make sure you don't forget any of your weak points, as well as making up many weak points you never had). They also can help supply the resources you may need to end the violence once and for all.

## Family Members

Battered wives often turn to their own family for help. Less commonly, they may contact members of their husband's family. Mothers tend to be the prime family helpers, followed by sisters, brothers and fathers. Even the women's own children were sometimes able to rescue them from beatings, but at great cost, as we shall see in Chapter 9. On the average, each request for help was met by seven or eight sessions or instances of help during the following month. Half of all the help received by battered women from their families was likely to be physical help, not just talking. Other common types of help that battered wives received were being told what they should do to end the violence, focused talking about the battering, direct intervention in the situation (such as by talking to the husband about his problem), and just listening. In addition, family members provided shelter away from the batterer, paid lawyers' fees or purchased plane tickets so the battered wife could escape, talked with her about how to deal with her husband, and helped her plan a new life without violence. The following excerpts illustrate both positive and negative aspects of battered wives' decisions to ask family members for help.

> The first time [the violence] was aimed at me, I left and got help from my family (mother and brother — I never told my father.)

> My family would not help me, always with the advice from my mother (during her third marriage), "hold your family (two children under eight) together."

> I have a wonderful set of parents who were more than willing to help me when I could take no more. They were never told about the abuse, although, only that I needed out.

> My dad has offered me a place to stay with him and my stepmother, but they have five of her children living with them now, and I know it would be pretty well cramped up.

> I have decided to leave the state and to live with my brother and his wife who said they will welcome me with open arms... I will be receiving a check from my Christmas Club and that is what I must use since all our bankbooks are kept under lock and key with my husband holding the only key.

> It has been a little over a year now that my husband

has stopped abusing me both physically and emotionally... Because of a friend who encouraged me to bring his behavior to the attention of our families, I have lived one year in peace. When our families found out the truth about my husband they were shocked with disbelief. They thought I was overexaggerating the circumstances and I was the one in need of mental help. Had it not been for a friend who supported me and my stories, I'm sure life would have continued as usual.

When young children try to defend their mother, the result can be child abuse. This was the case in two of the following three letters. In the third letter, an adult daughter was successful in preventing further damage to her mother.

> The boys tried to protect me many times, but he'd buy them off or hurt them also and the girls were too little. I can remember many times him telling them he wasn't hurting Mommy, just funning - and then he'd laugh. The kids would run [and] hide.

> [Once] I threatened him with a rifle. The rifle must have scared him. He didn't hit me for a long time. But too, our boys were getting old enough to protect me — if they needed to... When my husband held a pocket knife (very sharp) against my throat one time, I just knew he'd kill me. But my oldest son (then 15) came in on it and my husband let me go and took off his belt and whipped the boy. I ran!

> Last November he went on another rampage, hit me with a stray door, smashed a chair and hurled it at me so hard that another inch up would have fractured both kneecaps, tore the top of the newel post off the

stairs and was about to hurl it when my daughter came down (she rents the top floor apartment) and broke him up. [She] took him back to _____ [a clinic].

Battered wives are much less likely to approach their in-laws for help than their own family members, for good reason. If your in-laws think their son is always right, or if they accept wife-beating in their own marriage, you should not expect help from them.

In my research, when in-laws did help, mothers-in-law were the most likely source, with sisters-in-law and brothers-in-law being used somewhat less often. On the average, in-laws provided five different instances of help in response to each request for aid, spread over a period of a little more than a month. In-laws were more likely than members of the wives' own families to deal directly with the batterers, but they were much less likely to provide material aid and direct service to the battered women. The following two quotes are among the very few positive comments that were made about in-laws by the battered women in my research:

> Since filing for divorce, leaving the children with the father's family, the pain I endured has finally [turned] into relief.

> I called my husband's aunt, who I knew only slightly. She came to my rescue and took me and my two children (ages 3½ years and 6 months) to her house. My in-laws were semi-supportive, but since I was pregnant they were mainly interested in keeping the family together. He called, swore he'd never do it again. I felt I had no choice [but to return to him].

## Suggestions

It is always dangerous for a battered wife to contact her in-laws. Even if they take her part in the short run, they may shift ground later on. If the abuser were to be exposed in public, his parents would stand to suffer a great deal of family embarrassment. I once knew a battered wife who hid out in a friend's basement with her two young children for nearly a month while her husband ranted and raged. Then she made the mistake of talking with his mother. Although the mother-in-law appeared sympathetic, she violated the battered woman's trust and told her son the location of the hiding place. He immediately forced entry to the friend's house and recaptured his wife, not unlike the cartoons of a caveman dragging a desired mate home to his lair by her hair.

## Friends

Friends are important to women who are reaching out for help. Often they are more important than family members. You cannot select family members who are unsympathetic to your plight, but you have had an entire lifetime to develop friendships with people who hold values similar to your own. If your family is worried about keeping up appearances, they may not always give you the best advice. Friends will not be embarrassed if you become the first person in your family ever to file for a divorce or to expose your husband's violence in public.

When you ask your friends for help, you will probably be surprised by their willingness to pitch in on your behalf. The typical request for help by women in my research led to supportive services from a friend on eight separate occasions during the following three months. Friends did not limit their help to just talking about the problem in general or telling the battered wives what they should do to rid themselves of the violence. They also helped them in more concrete ways, providing shelter, transportation, cash, and referrals to helping professionals such as lawyers, counselors, women's groups, district attorneys, and the clergy. Here are a few of the ways friends can help.

Thanks to a dear, dear friend and her family, she helped me escape after advising me that one day he would eventually kill me.

I didn't leave for another year after I told a friend. But her reaction - very upset - made it possible for me to conceive of leaving. After that I began to see that I didn't deserve it and didn't have to stay.

A friend kept after me to leave my husband, or throw him out, just for a while at least, so we could straighten out our thinking and make some decisions. She finally made the decisions for me by calling the police for me one night...my husband had threatened me with a baseball bat.

A close and very supportive circle of friends helped me get through this, helped me hide out in their homes, [and] provided transportation.

...an argument started, he pushed me down on the bed and was going to hit me, if it hadn't been for a friend and my son.

## Suggestions

The most important theme expressed by battered women about the help they received from friends concerns the strong interpersonal support that enabled them to strengthen their self-confidence. Developing self-confidence is often a necessary first step before a battered woman can take appropriate action against her husband. Asking for help from a friend when one is being battered is one of the supreme tests of a friendship. Those friends who fail the test should find that their friendships are being reevaluated. If you ask a friend for help and she or he says no, you probably have only an acquaintance. In my experience, real friends at least try to help.

## Neighbors

Neighbors are the least frequently used informal sources of help. However, my research disclosed that once helping relationships were initiated with neighbors, they tended to help for a longer period of time than did family or in-laws. Perhaps this was because battered wives and their neighbors lived just a few steps apart. Like other informal help-sources, neighbors take considerable personal risk in becoming involved in a violent marriage. It is not uncommon for husbands to find out about the helping activities of neighbors and to threaten them if they persist. In a few of the case histories, the husbands physically assaulted neighbors who came to the aid of the beaten wives.

Another reason why a helping neighbor is in danger of assault by an enraged husband is that neighbors tend to become heavily involved with women who come to them for help. They do not limit themselves to verbal help. Instead, they tend to offer shelter, transporation, a willingness to call the police whenever violence occurs, first aid for injuries, child care, and cash. Some neighbors courageously confront the batterer with his behavior, and others indicate willingness to physically intervene with the batterer on behalf of his wife.

> I'm lucky to have found a friend in my neighbor. After 3½ years I've found someone who understands and is willing to listen to me. By accident, we found what we had in common, though not always pretty, we do have a kind of release.

> I have several neighbors whose husbands have either beaten them regularly or have attempted to beat them regularly.
>
> I have...a good neighbor who would help me with anything I need.

Help from neighbors reported by the women I interviewed included calling the police, offering safe shelter from the batterer, providing transportation to the hospital, watching for a signal that the wife was being attacked and then summoning help on her behalf, punching the batterer in defense of the wife, caring for the children, providing literature on family violence, and counseling the wife on how to end the violence in her life.

## Seeking Shelter

Many of the battered women in my research reported spousal abuse which occurred some years ago, long before the first battered women's shelter was opened. Even today, there is not a single country in which there are enough battered women's shelters to meet the need. Luckily, friends, neighbors, and family members are often willing to step forward and offer shelter to beaten wives, sometimes for many months.

One of every ten women, according to my research, took shelter away from her husband overnight or longer when she was battered for the first time. The use of sheltering rose steadily to three of every ten women by the final battering incident. The children generally accompanied their mothers into the sheltering situations. Most of the sheltering help came from the women's relatives, and substantial help also came from friends and neighbors. Only one out of every twenty sheltered women was helped by battered women's shelters and women's resource centers, so the current statistics on the use of battered women's shelters are just the tip of the iceberg. The average length of stay in a sheltering situation by the battered women was fifteen days. A number of women stayed away from their mates for six months or longer before deciding (usually under great pressure from their husbands) to come back and give it one more try. Besides providing physical protection from the batterers, the people giving shelter to the injured women helped by talking with them about what to do to prevent future assaults. These people also loaned or gave them money to see lawyers, obtain medical care, and pay living expenses.

My research indicates that public shelters provide only one-eighth of the sheltering received by battered women. Relatives were more than three times as likely as public shelters to shelter battered women, and friends were more than twice as likely to do so. Putting it another way, without friends and relatives, most abused wives would have no place to hide from their husbands' violence.

Sheltering is important for many reasons. First, it removes women from immediate danger. In the long run, however, most battered wives return home and are again exposed to their husbands' abusiveness. Sheltering can help women achieve permanent freedom from abuse if it scares or embarrasses husbands into reforming. It also helps battered women get away from their husband's coercion in order to assess their lives and their marriages. Taking shelter for several weeks is often the first step in the improvement of a battered woman's self-image. As she gains in strength and independence from her husband, she is laying the ground work for her own emancipation — in many cases not only from violence, but also from his jealous domination of every aspect of her life. I will explore the value of sheltering to battered wives more fully in Chapter 8.

## Comparing Informal Help-Sources

If you want to get help without contacting the police or a social agency, your best bets are friends and members of your own family. Battered women go to friends and their own family for help more than twice as often as they contact in-laws and neighbors. Family members are most likely to have an immediate positive effect on the husbands, and friends are not far behind. In-laws and neighbors are much less helpful. The long-term contributions made by these sources of help to the eventual termination of the violence are greater than their immediate effects on the batterers. These effects involve changes in the wife's self-image, her determination to become free of the violence, and her willingness to go to lawyers, counselors, the police and other powerful sources of help to end the battering.

Sheltering by friends and family members often leads to negative reactions by the husbands. Many husbands are severely threatened by the sheltering. It is an indication that their control over their wives is weakening. There is no doubt that the secret is out, at least to those who are providing the shelter. Threatened husbands may react with violence, threats of all kinds (to the people providing shelter as well as the battered wives), and other rational and irrational acts as they desperately try to get their wives back under their thumbs.

Don't be fooled if this happens to you. The more negatively your husband reacts, the more sure you can be that he is threatened by your new-found strength. Although this can be dangerous to you in the short run, it is a good sign that it may be possible for him to change his ways. In any case, it is better than the husbands who insincerely promise to end the violence in order to get their wives to come home, and then resume their assaultive behavior. *It is almost impossible to go wrong in taking shelter.* Looking back on all their various attempts to get their husbands to stop the beatings, the women in my research were nearly unanimous in their opinion that taking shelter made an important contribution to ending the violence.

Friends, neighbors and family members all make significant contributions to the lives of the battered women who come to them for help. Are they more helpful to some kinds of women than to others, or in one situation more than another? It is reassuring that the answer is no. It doesn't make much difference what your background is, what kind of husband you have, or how badly he abuses you. Help received from friends, neighbors and family members is useful to all kinds of women, and in all situations. So you will find your friends, family, and perhaps even neighbors and in-laws to be wonderful sources of help. All you have to do is ask them.

## Cautions

There are three cautions about using informal help that must be mentioned. The first, that family, friends and neighbors risk victimization when they help you, has been mentioned already. The other two cautions are legal entanglements and social complications. Legal entanglements occur when a friend, relative or neighbor witnesses your husband's abuse in a case that leads to criminal prosecution, if their house is cited in a restraining order, or when they otherwise become parties to some legal action that you bring against your husband. Legal entanglements usually mean that they must appear in court, and they are forced (almost always) to reveal their identity to the batterer. In rare cases, your husband may even try to take legal counteraction against them.

The social complications of intervention by friends, relatives and neighbors can be elaborate. For example, how will their involvement with you change their relationships with the batterer? The complications multiply if they offer you shelter for an extended period of time, especially if you bring children with you.

The best way to avoid wearing out your welcome is to discuss these matters openly so that you understand their feelings and they understand yours. In fact, it is only fair to discuss all three potential problems with anyone who offers to help you.

## Conclusion

The common sense assumption that battering situations require professional help in order to be resolved is an oversimplification. My research confirms the view that many battered women can become free of violence without the help of a professional counselor. Many of the women we interviewed who had ended the violence in their lives had no contact with social workers or other professionals with expertise in counseling. Furthermore, where such contacts with professionals occured, they were usually supplemented by extensive support services from friends, family, and neighbors. However, the more frequent and severe the batterings, the more likely it is that professional help is needed. If you are being abused by your husband, you may need expert help to deal with feelings of guilt, anger, depression, or other psychological problems that sometimes persist long after the violence has ended.

In addition, neighbors, friends and family, in contrast to professional counselors, do not always play the same role in defeating wife-beating and its negative consequences. One of the reasons why these women were beaten was that their husbands wanted to absolutely dominate them and their children. The batterers used psychological strategies to manipulate them, strategies that often resembled brainwashing in its most extreme form. Women subjected to physical and mental abuses for years often develop a negative opinion of themselves and are unlikely to have the self-confidence needed to regain control over their lives.

In summary, family, friends and neighbors along with battered women's shelters, women's groups, and professional counselors all can help battered women. They can help battered women improve their self-images to where they will once again determine their own courses of action. In fact, in several cases studied, support from family, friends and neighbors stimulated the battered women to enlist the aid of professionals and shelter houses, thereby increasing pressure on their husbands. The success of professionals and shelter house personnel was partly due to the personal growth and development that battered women achieved before contacting them.

# 4

# Lawyers and Physicians

Physicians and lawyers can help battered wives. However, they share a commitment to service delivery that is narrow. As might be expected, medical professionals are likely to focus on physical needs, not psychological, social, and legal needs. Lawyers usually confine their help to legal matters, while giving little attention to your other needs. Your other needs sometimes have legal implications, so your talks with lawyers may get into these areas. This can be an advantage, but it also can be a trap. Remember that most lawyers are not trained psychological therapists. While their legal advice may be good, their therapeutic advice may not be up to the standard established by professional therapists. The exceptions to this are those rare lawyers (most of them women) who have received formal training in therapy, who work closely with women's groups and battered women's shelters, or who have specialized in helping victimized women.

## Limitations of Medical Services

After an acute battering incident, abused women often require medical attention for their physical injuries. Medical personnel, especially those working in emergency rooms, may be the first people to whom these women have revealed their injuries. In spite of the epidemic of abused women seeking medical help, few are identified as being abused. Many studies have shown that few doctors and other medical personnel will ask in depth questions about how the woman was injured, even when it is obvious that the injuries could not have happened by accident. When battered women are too embarrassed to insist that the source of their injuries be recorded, many will take their cue and refrain from asking embarrassing questions.

Most physicians and nurses are primarily trained in the treatment of physical problems resulting from accidents, diseases, and the aging process. Wife-beating is fundamentally different because it is both a personal and a social problem. It cannot be treated by bandages and medicines alone. For this reason, battered women who are seen by physicians should be routinely referred to other sources of help.

Initially, questions about medical personnel were omitted in my research because I assumed that few physicians and nurses ever contributed significantly to the ending of a woman's victimization. However, a few comments about physicians by the battered women prompted me to gather data on medical personnel. Despite suffering serious assaults over and over, only 39 percent of the women reported receiving help from physicians or nurses following at least one battering. Only one out of twelve of these battered women found medical personnel to be effective in helping end her victimization, and only one out of four rated medical help as being even slightly effective. Physicians and nurses were, by and large, as effective with one type of battered woman as another. Furthermore, they were less effective in helping these women than other help-sources, such as social service agencies, lawyers, women's groups, and battered women's shelters. The following quotes illustrate the experiences that women had with physicians and nurses:

> After we separated I told him if we were to get back together he had to get counseling. He went three times to our family doctor (who is Baptist) who told

him to read the Bible and pray to God and I would come back to him. Our doctor told me I should have stayed in the marriage and I was rebelling at God by leaving the marriage.

I did talk briefly with my family Doctor. I told her, I have never been a quitter at anything. That I believed "through sickness and in health." I had offered to go to the hospital if my husband would take the alcohol abuse program. But my husband refused even though he knew he would lose his job. My Doctor said, you can't help him if he won't help himself. She told me, do now what is best for you.

I went to our family doctor and told him everything. My doctor prescribed a mild sedative and wrote a letter to my lawyer telling him that an emergency divorce would be beneficial for both my physical and mental health.

[The doctor was] there and when I mentioned [being] beaten up, he insulted me, humiliated me and said "leave." I said I'm scared, etc. He said each visit will be...$50...I went back...[and saw] a new young *sassy* doctor, and when I mentioned wife beating, [it] was [the] same. I'm sorry, you don't have $50 - don't come.

## Suggestions

When you see a physician for injuries related to your husband's abuse, be sure to ask that evidence be recorded which you could use if you ever decided to take legal action. This is even more important if your children are being treated for injuries inflicted on them by your husband. Some physicians and nurses will be sympathetic, others may be skeptical. You must be ready to be assertive in order to receive the treatment and the documentation you need, as well as any referrals that might be appropriate. Under present laws, the reporting of abused children seen by physicians and nurses has greatly improved. Battered wives should receive the same treatment.

## The Lawyer as Friend and Advisor

Most of the formerly battered women in my research contacted at least one lawyer during their journey toward a violence-free life. Each contact resulted in several sessions extending over a period of about three months. The lawyers gave the battered women the help they requested in about 75 percent of the cases. In the remaining contacts, they either gave verbal support instead of legal help, or they gave no support or help at all. The most common legal action requested by the battered wives was a divorce. Other kinds of legal aid requested included help in filing assault charges and petitions for a legal separation or a restraining order.

In our research, 43 percent of the battered women sought a lawyer. The women were more likely to use lawyers than physicians and nurses (39 percent), the clergy (33 percent), battered women's shelters (26 percent), and women's groups (21 percent), but less likely than social service or counseling agencies (50 percent) and the police (53 percent). These women gave their lawyers very high effectiveness ratings. Fifty percent felt their lawyers were "very effective" or "somewhat effective" in ending the violence against them. This is a higher rating than for any other formal source of help except women's groups and battered women's shelters. Let us see what battered wives say about their lawyers, both positively and negatively.

> I went to my lawyer. [The batterer] sobered up almost immediately and got into a long term treatment program.

My case seems to be unique and my attorney [is] at a loss, not to mention an indifferent court system... the emotional strain...has made me realize that our court system is often based on the personal feelings of a judge which leaves me and the rest of the battered women of this county with no place to turn for protection.

All lawyers are interested in is money "up front" and *lots* of it.

Went to a lawyer and found out I can get a "Restraining Order" and can sue him, but not without proof. So next time I get a black eye, fat lip or hair pulled out I will go to police or hospital for documentation.

My lawyer was very supportive. Initially, his outrage at the way I had been treated was very helpful for me to express and justify my own anger. My lawyer served as an advisor, encouraging me to make my own decisions. He was very helpful without being domineering or authoritarian.

## Suggestions

Before you contact a lawyer, make up your mind about whether you want to follow through on legal action against your husband, or whether you merely want to scare him into improving his behavior. If you only want to scare him and this appears to be effective in motivating him to control his violence, it is best to drag things out as much as possible (assuming that you can afford whatever charges are involved). On the other hand, if you have decided to follow through on a legal action regardless of your husband's short-term reaction, you should move as quickly as possible toward the successful conclusion of the prosecution, divorce or legal separation. Unnecessary delays only increase the chances of further beatings and give your husband time to entangle you in legal hassles that will limit your freedom.

Lawyers are ready to act as your agent. They give advice when they are asked. They help you reach your legal goals after you have explained what you want. You must be assertive when you see a lawyer. Once you have decided what you would like your future to be, then it is time to bring in a lawyer to take care of the legal details and to advise you of the best way to protect your interests. Since some lawyers are far better than others at helping battered wives, seek referrals from battered women's shelters, women's organizations, crisis lines, friends, relatives, and anyone else you know. Identify lawyers who are *both* competent and sympathetic to the plight of abused women.

Lawyers are further from the source of legal power than district attorneys, but they know how to get the law on the side of the battered wife. A good divorce lawyer can often have more impact on a violent husband than the police.

It is best to continue legal action against your husband until you feel sure that he has permanently changed his behavior toward you. It is better to deactivate the legal process instead of terminating it, and to leave the door open to reactivating it if he beats you again.

## Evaluating Your Marriage

Deciding whether to involve the law in your marriage should be based on a careful evaluation of your situation. Ask yourself these questions:

- Does your husband try to undermine your self-confidence every time he gets a chance?

- Does he force sex on you against your will? If he does, you should consider this rape.

- Does he sometimes beat your children too?

- Does he show any pleasure in your suffering?

- Does he have friends who support his beating you, or who beat their wives?

- Has he ever beaten you while you were pregnant?

- Have you ever been beaten so badly that you had to go to the doctor or a hospital?

- Are you afraid that he might assault friends or relatives if they were to help you hide out after a beating?

- Do you believe that he might seriously or permanently injure you or the children at some time in the future?

- Do you believe that he is committed to violence as a way of solving his problems and controlling you?

- Has his violence against you continued for a long period of time?

- Does your husband beat you every time you try to have some life of your own apart from his domination (for example, having a close friend, taking a night class, or being in a bowling league)?

The more "yes" answers to these questions, the worse your

marriage. It doesn't really matter whether you still love him, have a good sex life much of the time, and find many good days between beatings. You can't live a normal life with a man who behaves like this — even some of the time. It also doesn't matter why you think he is violent with you. Perhaps he had a poor upbringing, has a drinking problem, is out of work, has a bad temper, or feels inferior to you. These excuses won't help him in court if you file assault charges, and they probably won't help you at home if you continue to make allowances for his behavior. You don't need to be a psychologist to know that adults must be responsible for their own behavior. It is his responsibility to end his abusive behavior. Your responsibility to yourself and your children will lead you to take steps to improve your situation if he doesn't change his behavior.

The more "yes" answers to these questions, the more seriously you should consider following through on legal action against your husband, not just scaring him. Divorce is an extremely serious step, but it should not be ruled out. It is always available as an option when other strategies fail, or when your husband has so thoroughly destroyed his relationship with you that you no longer wish to live with him even if he never beats you again. Do not hesitate to tell your lawyer, the police, or the district attorney the full details of your husband's behavior. It is embarrassing, but you can't expect them to give your case the attention it deserves when you hold back facts.

# 5
# Law Enforcement

When you ask your friends for help after a battering incident, they may be able to help you. However, friends usually will not cause your husband to change his behavior. Even if they choose to talk with him about the violence, they have no power to compel him to stop beating you. The same thing is true of family members, neighbors, and counselors. Only when violent husbands are drawn into counseling with their spouses or join a therapy group for batterers can counselors directly influence them.

The services offered to battered wives by the police and district attorneys differ in three ways from the help available elsewhere. First, they both have legal power. They need not merely suggest that a husband stop beating his wife. They can demand that he do so, and can threaten him with imprisonment and other powerful punishments if he disobeys.

Second, police and district attorneys differ from most other sources of help for battered wives by dealing directly with violent husbands. Their activities are not limited to helping battered wives gain the strength to do something to better protect themselves from their violent spouses. Instead, police and district attorneys get at the source of the violence. The full weight of their legal power can come to rest squarely on the shoulders of the batterers. Their effect on the batterers can be immediate. This leads to the point that legal and law enforcement actions differ from other helping activities in that they are public, not secret. Husbands who are arrested and charged with a crime can no longer hide their abusiveness from view. For middle and upper class batterers, publicity may be a stronger threat than imprisonment.

## Who To Call?

Police calls by battered wives are unlikely to be well thought out. Afraid for their lives, these women want physical protection from continued violence. When the police are called, it is usually while the beatings are in progress rather than between beatings. Hence, it is a crisis situation in which careful planning is impossible. This is even more likely when neighbors or other outsiders call the police. When the police are called by a person uninvolved in the violence, their arrival on the scene is as much of a surprise to the battered wives as to their husbands.

The effect calling the police might have on your husband is an important consideration. If you've called the police before, you have a good idea of how your husband will react when you call them again. If you are facing your first police call in the near future, you can get a hint about how your husband will react by recalling how he has reacted when the police gave him traffic tickets, or how he has reacted to other contacts with people in authority. If you conclude that your husband will beat you up even worse in retaliation for calling the police, that does not mean that you should continue to tolerate his abuse. In this case, you should consider the possibility of leaving him immediately, taking your children with you, and seeking shelter elsewhere while you obtain a restraining order, a legal separation, or a divorce.

Making an appointment to see someone in the district attorney's office is not something that is done in the middle of a beating. Women have time to consider their situations while they are healing from previous beatings, and are able to carefully decide what to do. Do not begin a case with the district attorney unless you intend to stay with it until the case is decided in court. It is wasteful if you drop the charges after the district attorney's office has already put much time and effort into your case. And it decreases the chances that the district attorney will take your case or other battered women seriously in the future. Although it is your right to drop the charges, the district attorney will not appreciate your doing so. You should also be aware that some jurisdictions have new domestic violence laws allowing the district attorney to continue legal action against your husband even if you want to withdraw the charges.

## When The Police Arrive

Women in my research who had been severely beaten for years were more likely than the average battered wife to have had contacts with the police. Seven of every eight police calls were made by the wives. Neighbors and friends made most of the remaining calls. The main reason the battered wives called the police was fear for their lives. Another common reason for calling the police was that they wanted to impress their husbands with their seriousness about ending the violence.

When called, the police officers in my research generally arrived at the scene of the crime within ten to fifteen minutes of the call for help. Unfortunately, in only half of the cases the officers provided an identifiable service to the battered wives. Most of the help the women received from the police consisted of either forcing the husbands to temporarily end the abuse, or offering the victim material aid such as transportation to a hospital or to a place of shelter. In one out of every ten calls, the police offered verbal support through talking or listening instead of doing something directly to end the violence. Here are some examples of the services that police officers provided to the battered wives.

[The police] stood out on my front lawn and allowed us to be beaten...with a lead pipe knowing we were all in here helpless, including my son [who was] 6 years at that time.

He had smashed jars of baby food all over the kitchen and kicked in a door and hit me numerous times. When the police arrived he became the perfect gentleman. They informed me I would have to go to the police station to file a report, they couldn't arrest him on the spot. I had to beg them not to leave me alone. I called my husband's aunt, who...came to my rescue...

I dropped assault charges, telling the police [my husband] was only under stress. The police had urged me not to, because they said it will happen again, that we all have stress, but another human being can't be the punching bag...

Before the police had gotten to our apartment my husband had threatened me with a baseball bat, and I took off in our car. I returned a few hours later and found he had been asked [by the police] to go to his parents' home...

I finally called the police last month when he refused to give me my children after a fight...The police only got my children and let me get what I needed to leave with. All they said was leave him and don't go back. It's so easy to say that.

...I was three months pregnant and got slapped, kicked and punched. I was thrown on the bed and had hair torn out and attempted strangulation — luckily the cops arrived then — a neighbor heard us and called them.

When he became violent, I had the police throw him out, many times, but he would break back in again.

The battered wives I interviewed usually asked the police to arrest their husbands, but the police complied with only one out of every six arrest requests. Police officers were most likely to respond by trying to talk the wife into working out her differences with her husband, or by claiming that she had no case and openly refusing to make an arrest. Once the police left the house, they rarely had any further contact with the battered wife. There were only a few cases in which the police stopped in or subsequently contacted the battered wives to see how they were doing or to offer additional help.

## Calling The District Attorney

Less than one out of three formerly battered women in my research made direct contact with the district attorney's office to file criminal charges against their husbands. Those who did had already made up their minds that nothing other than prosecution for assault would end their husbands' violence. Their experiences with district attorneys were similar to their experiences with lawyers in private practice. Although some of the women encountered indifference or disbelief, most of them were pleased with the power of the law to force their husbands to become less violent. The battered wives followed through on just over half of the cases filed with the district attorney's office, as compared with less than a third of the legal actions initiated through lawyers in private practice. The following vignettes illustrate what can happen when you seek help from a district attorney.

[The District Attorney] dropped the aggravated assault charge because I was too scared to appear in court.

Charges have been filed [and] he will receive time in jail if I and the county attorney have anything to do about it.

He brought a hatchet into my house and attacked my boyfriend in front of my children. The law is useless. He was charged with assault and the charge was reduced to "disorderly conduct" and he was fined $20.

The judge gave him six months, [to] come and go [on] work release, on charges of assault with intent to do great bodily harm...This man already had previous records in four states.

## A Comparison

Police, lawyers, and district attorneys provide different services to battered women, and their contacts occur at different points in the battering cycle. Formerly battered women made two sets of ratings of the police, lawyers, and district attorneys, both concerning whether they really helped end the battering. The first ratings were of the husband's immediate reaction. Did he stop beating his wife because she saw a lawyer, or did he step up the violence to keep her in line? The second set of ratings involved the long-term successfulness of the help received. This differs from the husband's immediate reaction, measuring the contribution of the help received to the eventual permanent ending of the violence.

### The Husband's Reaction

According to the battered wives, their husbands' immediate reactions to the police were more likely to be negative than positive. Negative reactions included being verbally abusive to both the police and the wife; threatening the wife with increased violence if she followed through on the complaint; laughing with the police about the "naughty" wife; and/or pretending calmness until the police left, followed by continued violence. In only about 25 percent of the cases did the husband calm down and agree to stop beating his wife.

This dismal situation is partly caused by the nature of police intervention in family violence. The police arrive during a crisis when emotions are high, and they rarely stay at the scene of the crime long enough to permit things to truly calm down. Police officers are also unlikely to have the skills to help battering husbands come to grips with their violent tendencies, and they would be in trouble with their superiors if they took the time to do so. Husbands and wives both know that the police will soon leave, after which there is no way for the police to protect anyone from futher intimidation and violence.

The best way to break this pattern of police ineffectiveness, given the inadequacies of the criminal justice system, is for police officers to temporarily remove the husband or escort the wife from the home in every case in which there is a reasonable chance of continued violence or intimidation. If the wife chooses to leave, she may wish to go to a hospital, a battered women's shelter, or another place of refuge. Should she prefer to stay, her husband can be taken to the police station to cool off, or to be booked if she has filed a criminal complaint against him.

Lawyers and district attorneys, in our research, were much more likely than police officers to have a positive short-term effect on the violent husbands. Nearly two-thirds of the batterers apologized and ended the abuse (at least for the time being) when they heard that their wives were consulting lawyers or filing charges with the district attorney. An additional one-fifth of the husbands promised to end the beatings forever if their wives would drop their cases and have nothing more to do with the legal system.

## Success In The Long Run

Police officers' contribution to the eventual ending of the violence was greater than their immediate effect on the husband, but they were still less effective than lawyers. Somewhat more than one-third of the formerly battered wives in our study rated the help received from the police and from district attorneys as "very effective" or "somewhat effective," as compared with half of the women who received help from lawyers in private practice or legal aid clinics.

This is no surprise, for help from lawyers often extends over a long period of time, while the police rarely follow up even once on a domestic violence call. The police can only contribute to the permanent end of the violence when their impact on the batterer, during a single visit of fifteen minutes to half an hour, is so forceful that he is afraid to beat his wife again.

There are at least three explanations for the relative neglect of battered wives by district attorneys in the past. First, domestic violence has been historically defined as a private, not public, criminal matter. Second, district attorneys believe that battered wives are less likely than many other victims to follow through on the prosecution of the criminal. There is also the point that even if the battered wives follow through, juries and judges sometimes do not convict offenders in these cases, and district attorneys prefer convictions.

However, attitudes are changing rapidly. The number of victim-witness support programs is increasing. They will provide special attention and help, including even such details as providing child care and transportation when a battered woman appears in court. Many states and provinces have recently passed domestic violence laws that have increased the legal protection for wives, facilitating the successful prosecution of violent husbands. These laws will also probably increase the proportion of judges who are willing to take a strong position against wife-batterers. Judges and prosecuters are finding out that when battered women receive adequate support services, they are unlikely to drop the charges against their abusers.

## Recommendations

There are few institutions that are more completely dominated by men and by male values than the law. Women represent only a small proportion of police officers, lawyers, prosecuting attorneys, and judges in western civilization. Even when women manage to work their way into the system, they are usually excluded from positions of influence and leadership. It is only recently that the first woman in history was appointed to the United States Supreme Court. Despite this, there are steps that battered women can take to maximize the value of the services they receive under the law.

If you think that you might need to call the police sometime, it is a good idea to write their phone number next to each telephone in the house. When you need them, you might not have time to look up their number in the phone book. It is also helpful to have a phone put in a bedroom or another room in which you can lock yourself while you call for aid. A bedroom phone can be justified to your husband as a safety device, so you can call for help if you ever hear a burglar while he is away.

Getting help from a lawyer or the prosecuting attorney is easier to accomplish, since you can call when your husband is out of the house. A visit to their offices can be disguised as a shopping trip or a visit to a friend or relative. Be sure that the friend or relative is willing to back up your story before you mention it to your husband. He may call to check on you.

There is no choice of police officers or prosecuting attorneys. You get whom they give you, and you have to hope that the person is attentive, sympathetic and competent.

If you are not satisfied with your lawyer, you can seek legal help elsewhere. You can go back to step one of the search process and get recommendations for a new lawyer. With the police and district attorneys, it is harder to change who you have, so an even greater stress must be placed on being assertive. Be polite. Try to control your emotions so that you are not labelled as hysterical. Present all the facts you can in support of your request for help. And, above all, insist on your rights. The key word in dealing with the law is assertiveness.

The quality of services to battered women by the police and prosecutors is rising so rapidly that you will probably have a better experience with the law than did many of the women in my research. Should you be disappointed with the services offered, remember that you can always file complaints. Prosecutors can be reported to the local association of lawyers and to the court.

There also may be police review board that accepts complaints about police officers. A few successful complaints filed by battered women will have an effect on police policies and the behavior of police officers who answer domestic violence calls. Prosecuting attorneys are sensitive to public opinion about how well they are doing their jobs.

In addition to these ways of insisting on your own legal rights, be sure to remember to pass along to other women information about the treatment you have received. Crisis lines, women's groups, shelters, and other women's organizations need to hear about your good experiences as well as your bad experiences so they can give better advice to other battered women.

# 6

# Counseling and Therapy Services

There are three basic sources of counseling for battered women and many differing approaches within each basic source. The three main sources are the clergy; social service and counseling agencies; and women's groups. If you think you have a serious emotional problem, a psychologist (sometimes called a clinical psychologist), a social case worker or a psychiatrist may be what you need (or what your abuser needs). If your emotional health is not much of a problem, a member of the clergy may be helpful. Increasingly they are being trained in counseling. The clergy are included in this discussion because their main service to battered women is usually some form of counseling therapy. Indeed, the counseling they offer is often directly competitive with counseling in traditional social service agencies and community mental health centers. Some clergy are closely integrated with the social service system, while others are not.

On the other hand, if your problem is that your mate abuses you, and you want to plan a violence-free future, you may not need a therapist. A counselor specializing in helping wife-beating victims (and the victims of other crimes against women) may be better. Women's groups, battered women's shelters, women's centers, and feminist therapy centers are the places to go to find a counselor who specializes in helping battered women. If it turns out that you need a therapist, these women's counseling and support organizations will refer you to one. The next chapter examines their services in more detail.

Although, as we shall see, counseling in women's groups is very different from counseling in social service agencies, many women's groups are sponsored by these agencies.

## Social Service Agencies

Social service agencies may be public (supported by the government) or private. This difference is not as clear as it seems, for many private agencies derive much of their income from contracts to provide services to the clients of government supported agencies. In addition, some private agencies are sponsored and supported by religious groups. In my research, the average request for help from a social service agency resulted in sixteen sessions or other separate instances of help a spread over the following seven months. Often, the women participated in three dozen or more sessions, and received help for at least a year and a half.

When you contact a social service agency for help (regardless of whether it is a community mental health center, marital counseling program, family welfare clinic, or some other type of organization), the main form of help you should expect is talking about the problem with someone who is a professionally trained counselor. You may see a social worker, a psychologist, or another helping services professional.

The two main kinds of verbal help that they may give you are sometimes called directive and nondirective. In nondirective counseling, the counselor does not tell you what to do. He or she listens to what you have to say about the problem and helps you consider what you want to do. Because you have the strength within you to beat wife-beating, the counselor works to bring out your strength and supports you as you carry out your self-made plans to become free of violence.

Directive counseling involves a different method. You may

be questioned until the therapist has a clear picture of the problem. Then the therapist offers suggestions for solving it. Some therapists may even go so far as to forcefully tell you what they think you must do to end the violence in your life. Either directive or nondirective counseling can be helpful. Which you choose is up to you. If you know what kind of counseling you want, it is wise to say so when you phone for an appointment. Many counselors do both directive and nondirective counseling, so they can provide you with any mix of directive and nondirective help that you desire. When one agency can't give you what you want, they can refer you to another agency that has just what you are looking for.

Individual counseling or therapy means that you and the therapist are the only two people in the room. She or he gives you full attention. In group therapy, several people with similar problems meet with one or more therapists. You are likely to get more advice from other group members than from the therapist, who may be called the group leader or facilitator. Because they are going through similar crises in their lives, the other group members can offer you surprisingly good advice. You do not have to worry about your private life becoming public knowledge. Everyone in the group agrees not to repeat what is said there.

The most serious problem in the effectiveness of family violence counselors or therapists is that they rarely see the source of the problem—the man who abuses you. You can tell a counselor about your husband, but that is not the same as having your husband come along with you. Counselors may give bad advice because what you can tell them about your husband is not enough for them to be able to give you their best advice. Besides, if your husband is to change, he needs to be directly exposed to counselors and other helping professionals. The two of you can see a counselor together, the same counselor at different times, or separate counselors. All of these arrangements can help end the batterings.

Although counselors can help you understand your husband's behavior, and may be able to help you change him into a less violent mate, their primary contribution to your welfare lies elsewhere. *Their strongest point is their ability to help you clarify your goals and then to decide how you want to go about reaching them.* In addition, they can help you understand yourself—in particular, why you have chosen to deal with your husband in one way rather than another. Their final contribution is that they will care about you as a human being and be your ally in the battle against both physical and psychological abuse. Their supportiveness will help you improve your self-image. As you grow in strength and knowledge, you will be able to see your way clear to the end of the tunnel.

Here is what some battered women have said about their experiences with social service counselors and psychologists. Both negative and positive examples are included.

> When I went to a mental clinic for help, the Doctor which was a man, made me feel as though I was the one with the mental problem and suggested I use tranquilizers.

> I went to social services. They sent a social worker with me to visit him in jail. This social worker told him that the only way he could get out of jail (a bluff) was to agree to therapy. Of course he agreed as he wasn't fond of jail. We attended marriage counseling four times. For starters, after spending two hours with my husband, the therapist told us we were wasting time and money as my husband wasn't being honest.

> It was a long journey and I thank God I was able to afford therapy as I feel it was the final force that led me to leave him. I recognized that something was wrong and entered counseling against his wishes a-

lone (he went a few times—sort of as a cosmetic cover up—screaming "this is for truck drivers—not *Doctors*" or "everything would be alright if you'd just *conform* or learn to *obey* me").

We've tried counselors through the county and they weren't too great. We are now seeing a professional psychologist, provided to us through our church and a slight glimmer of hope to what seemed a dead end road. I was heavily leaning towards a divorce—the counselor doesn't encourage us to go either way—but I'm learning that I'm *not* the cause of his hitting me and my husband is learning what's triggering his anger.

I have been in therapy for two years—it literally saved my life. I have my own sense of self. My husband no longer beats me — *had better not*.

My counselor was wonderful! I have forgiven myself for staying with this batterer. I am able to see men (even sexually) and not feel the fear.

## The Clergy

Some ministers, priests and rabbis have taken special training in counseling techniques. Some may even have a counseling degree in addition to their religious training. However, most of the clergy do not have extensive counseling training, and almost none have taken special courses on family violence. When you go to the clergy for help, you are likely to receive a mixture of religious teachings and counseling. You may find that certain topics can't be discussed fully. For example, divorce, or even permanent separation, may be dismissed as unworthy of careful consideration.

In the past, many women were told to return home and do their religious duty, to turn the other cheek instead of calling the police when beaten, and to try harder to please their husband so they would be battered less frequently. However, recent years have seen more ministers, priests and rabbis whose counseling techniques resemble those of secular counselors. They will help you psychologically instead of interpreting their religious position to you.

In shopping for a secular counselor, you can choose widely. In any medium-sized or large city, you can choose among social workers, psychoanalysts, psychologists and psychiatrists. Perhaps you'd prefer a female over a male counselor, or a feminist over a traditionalist. All these possibilities are available to you, and you can get advice about which counselors are most appropriate for your needs by asking friends and relatives, or by calling a women's crisis line, women's service organization such as NOW, battered women's shelter, or any large community mental health center.

The situation is different with the clergy. You probably won't want to choose widely. You will go to your own minister or priest because you have established a good relationship with him over the years. That's right, I said *him* because nearly every minister and all priests are men. Your minister or priest might be a fine man, but that doesn't mean that he will be a good marriage counselor, particularly where violence is involved. If you want religious counseling and suspect that your minister or priest is not right for you, don't give up. Any priest or minister will be glad to see you. You don't have to be in a particular parish or congregation. If you shop hard enough, you can even find a female minister, and you can certainly locate a male minister who is knowledgeable about and sympathetic to the needs of women.

Priests, ministers and rabbis, like all people, vary in their skills and attitudes. The same people who can find a good psychologist or lawyer for you will also be able to recommend an appropriate member of the clergy for you to see.

The women in my study of formerly battered women received eleven separate counseling sessions or instances of help. These sessions occurred every week or so for approximately four months. The clergy generally helped them by talking about the problem in a nondirective way, or by providing concrete directions about what they should do to improve their situation. In addition to these helping behaviors, there were several instances of direct intervention, material aid, and other forms of physical involvement on their behalf. Many of the clergy were not shy about "getting their hands dirty" and helping out in whatever way the women needed most, even when it meant risking assault from a violent or enraged husband.

Among the battered women who were not helped, the story is different. The five quotes below are typical of the positive and negative experiences the battered women had with the clergy. Most of their quotes are negative because few of them made complementary remarks about their clergy in their letters.

> A clergyman suggested that "Maybe I wasn't pleasing my husband in bed," and that was why he beat me. Then I went to our priest (not the same one I talk to now). We talked about it but he was so much older—I guess maybe he was uncomfortable talking about it. He seemed so surprised — he had known my husband's family for years.

> When I left my husband years ago, I met with great opposition my decision to divorce him from ...church leaders... However, I never fully lost the fearfulness of men...

Many church leaders advocate staying in a marriage no matter how destructive or abusive the situation is. I too tried the positive-loving attitude — but none of this suited my ex-husband. I was the submissive wife because of my religious convictions, but the more submissive I became the more brutal and cruel my husband became.

The feeling I got from our church was that I was to suffer in silence. (Since we have separated they will not associate with me.)

## Getting Your Husband To A Counselor

Wife-beating is an unusual problem in that the counseling that most benefits the battered wife is counseling in which she doesn't participate at all — counseling that is received by her husband. It is extremely difficult to convince a batterer to sincerely participate in therapy designed to wean him from his violence. In my experience, most participation in counseling by batterers is superficial and dishonest. The battered wife must not only convince her husband to attend counseling sessions, she must also persuade him to take counseling seriously. The successful women in my research found that merely talking with their husbands or extracting promises from them did not produce satisfactory results. Threatening public exposure, divorce or prosecution was far more effective in getting their husbands to counselors. Some men attended counseling sessions under court orders as a condition of probation after their wives were successful in bringing their cases to court.

*Success is likely only when batterers "voluntarily" enter therapy* because their wives or others who are important to them have convinced them that they have a problem which must be solved for the marriage to remain intact. Forced participation gives counselors a brief opportunity to make the same case, but we cannot expect them to be successful very often where the batterers' own wives have failed. Under these circumstances, the batterer's participation will probably be brief as well as superficial and dishonest.

A final step in the successful treatment of a batterer is to expose him to the most effective counseling techniques. Practically nothing is known about what works best in counseling batterers because it has only been during the past few years that batterers have been identified as a distinct client group. There is currently an emphasis on teaching anger control techniques in many programs for batterers. I suspect that although anger training is useful, it deals with a symptom, not the fundamental cause of wife-beating. I predict that we will eventually pull together evidence to show that the most effective counseling for batterers (that is to say, counseling that is most likely to lead to permanent freedom from violence) will focus on changing their definitions of the value and rights of women, and reducing their need to dominate their wives and children.

How should you treat your husband while he is in therapy? This is a delicate matter. He will need understanding and support if he is really confronting the inappropriateness of his behavior and trying to remake his approach to family life. There will probably be some backsliding, which should not be allowed to ruin his self-image as someone who is making progress. The tricky part is to maintain this positive definition of the situation while simultaneously remaining steadfast in your opposition to his violence. If you do not maintain pressure on him, he can easily return to his old ways.

# 7
# Women's Groups

Women's groups are organized by women for women. These groups are devoted to solving problems faced by women in our society, one of which is wife-beating. Women's groups may be staffed by social workers or other professional counselors. More often, they are led by women who have been successful at solving problems themselves. With their help, the women in the group exchange experiences and advice, gradually moving toward solutions with which each of them feels comfortable. Through this process, women build their inner strength, their courage, and more positive self-images. Some women's groups are strongly feminist, but most of them are not. They reflect the values of the group members, so all can feel at home in the group discussions.

Women's groups are sponsored by Alanon and Alcoholics Anonymous, local churches, battered women's organizations, feminist groups, and shelters. Your own community is bound to have at least one such group unless it is quite small. Contacts with women's groups by the women I studied led to extensive help, averaging nineteen sessions over a period of more than eight months. Many women regularly attended these groups for a year and a half or more.

The kinds of help offered by women's groups are different from those provided by social service counseling agencies. The primary form of help I found being given in women's groups was modeling. In modeling, the group leader or group members tell about their experiences. The person whose problem is being discussed learns what she might do about it by hearing what others did when they had the same or a similar problem. Through this process, she also gains confidence that the problem can be solved. After all, other women just like her worked it out, so she can too.

There was little nondirective counseling in these women's groups, and even less directive counseling. A women's group leader and other group members may not tell another participant how she should solve her problem. They may talk instead about what worked for them. Whether it is wise for one to follow others' examples depends on how closely your circumstances resemble each other's. The decision to actually follow their example is entirely the individual woman's because the group respects the right of each to live her own life and her ability to make her decisions. Once she decides what to do, or if she has emergency needs, the group may be able to help with material aid such as transportation, child care, and shelter. Also the group may intervene directly with the criminal justice system to assure that satisfactory services are received from the police or the district attorney. Women's groups were about twice as likely as social service agencies and the clergy to provide material aid to the battered women. The outstanding effectiveness of women's groups is reflected in these quotes from letters written by the battered wives.

> I came upon a group three years ago called [a women's group]. They in turn helped me soooo much. I finally was told about the wife abuse program [nearby]. They helped me realize I was a "person" and I began to stand on my own two feet and gain the confidence I needed to leave.

For a long time I was convinced that I was crazy, a trouble-maker and the cause of unexplainable catastrophies of every sort... The hardest step was to pick up the telephone, and you don't know how happy I am that I did.

I was a battered wife, and after many crisis counseling calls to [a women's group] and a traumatic struggle to build up my non-existent self esteem, I am now divorced with custody of my two minor children.

We belong to a support group now — our county has [a number of] women's groups, there's one going for young girls now — I am so thankful, they have helped me look at this, my life. I am getting counseling in voicing fears and feelings that I was taught to suppress for years. I am a woman and I am proud of it, for so many years I just felt like I was being used or dirty. I am so happy to be able to say if I know someone who is hurting, I can help. I listen or I'll take you to someone who will.

I am writing in behalf of my Monday night support group. Our group is made up of battered wives... Our shelter has not been fully put together yet but we hope to aid many women in the years to follow.

## Reactions of Husbands

If your husband finds out that you are in counseling or therapy, he may be threatened and react negatively. He may assault you "to teach you a lesson" and demand that you immediately withdraw. Although you may be in danger from his violent behavior, a negative reaction from your husband could prove beneficial in the long run. If he is threatened enough to react strongly now, he may be willing to eventually compromise with you as you grow in strength and determination.

Husbands in my research reacted most positively to social service agency counseling and least positively to the clergy, with women's groups falling in between. Their positive reactions to social service agencies consisted mainly of agreeing to participate in treatment with their wives. Positive reactions to the clergy and women's groups were more likely to involve apologizing and agreeing to avoid battering their wives in the future. Negative reactions by husbands to all three sources of counseling included assaulting their wives to reestablish their control of the marriage, laughing at their wives' involvement as useless, and promising to end the violence only if their wives agreed to immediately drop out of counseling.

Women's groups are more likely than other counseling sources to make a contribution to permanently ending the violence, followed at some distance by social service/counseling agencies and the clergy. The women I studied confirmed the impressive effectiveness of women's groups as compared with other sources of counseling help. The long-term effectiveness of women's groups reflects both husbands who are threatened at first but eventually improve and women whose growth through their counseling experiences gradually gives them the confidence they need to convince their husbands that the violence must end if they are to remain married.

Battered women are unlikely to be successful in negotiations with their husbands unless they know that they have already become strong enough to make a break with their previous lives and live alone if their husbands refuse to stop abusing them.

## Finding Counseling Services

Counselors and other therapists are listed in the yellow pages of your telephone book under such headings as "human service organizations," "marriage and family counselors," "social workers," "social service agencies," and "psychologists." Psychiatrists may be listed under "physicians and surgeons - doctors of medicine." Women's groups are not usually listed separately. They often are mixed in with other social service organizations. Some women's groups are not listed at all. You can reach them by calling a women's center (like the YWCA), crisis hotline, or battered women's shelter. The clergy can be found in the listing of churches. Clergy who have a separate counseling practice will also be listed as psychologists, marriage and family counselors, or one of the other counseling classifications. Some phone books have a special emergency section containing numbers for police, fire stations, and services to families in distress, including crisis lines and other sources of help for battered women and abused children.

Unless you live in a very small town, there will be many therapists, clergy members and social agencies listed in the yellow pages. How do you choose among them? The best way to deal with this problem is to ask your friends and relatives what they have heard about counselors and women's groups and to call your local crisis line. Crisis lines operate 24 hours a day. They are staffed by people who are trained to refer you to the best source of help. All you have to do is tell them what help you need, or what problem you want help in solving. Existing agencies also make referrals to other sources of help, so you can call practically any counselor or agency and be referred to an appropriate help-source if there is no crisis line in your town. Battered women's shelters and other women's organizations are particularly good sources of information. Most agencies have sliding fee schedules, meaning counseling is either free or inexpensive for women who do not have much money. Battered women's groups are sometimes free to all women. Don't ever hold back from getting help because you think you can't afford it. If you look around, you can always find the help you need at a fee you can afford, even if that fee is zero.

## Recommendations

Women who have been battered for years may have temporarily lost the self-confidence they need to end the violence in their lives and to plan for the future. Therapists can be very helpful to battered women as they put their lives back together, whether this means leaving the batterer or staying in the family and trying to get him to end his violent behavior and his insistence on dominating them. The most important rule for judging the therapeutic services of the clergy and social service agencies is to find a therapist who helps you to feel better about yourself. If someone makes you feel worse about yourself, don't return after the second session. Go back to the beginning of the search process and identify another therapist who is known to be sympathetic to the plight of battered women.

In my research I found that counselors were about equally successful with all types of women. There was no single type of counseling that was much better for blacks than for whites, for the wealthy over the poor or for the educated over the less educated. Women's groups are an unusually effective counseling source for all types of battered women. However, it could be that in your community the best battered women's counselor is a member of the clergy. National statistics can never tell you what will be true of each counselor you meet. You should not rule out any counseling source in your own community until you have learned more about it.

Women's groups were rated by the battered women I studied as more helpful than any other source of counseling. The battered wives received an impressive amount of help from professionals who had advanced degrees in counseling, but they also received a great deal of help from women who had less professional education. Because they do not require highly-paid professionals and an elaborate administrative apparatus, women's groups are relatively inexpensive to operate.

Battered women in every city and town need more sources of help. In view of the effectiveness and low cost of women's groups most of the new counseling services created for battered women should be women's groups. This probably will not happen unless women begin to organize and demand that more resources be devoted to women's needs, and that battered women's shelters, groups, and service agencies be assigned top priority for government funding.

# 8
# Battered Women's Shelters

When a home becomes a horror, the only place to go is out. Sooner or later, most women who continue to be battered will be forced to seek temporary shelter away from the batterer. For some of these women, shelter will be provided by friends and relatives. For others, battered women's shelters are the only haven from an abusive and possibly life threatening situation.

## How To Find a Battered Women's Shelter

Perhaps you've only been battered a few times and without serious injury. You think you'll never need a battered women's shelter. That's the way most of the women I studied began, but the batterings didn't stop. They became worse over the years, and one day the women had to flee for their lives. It is better to plan now for that terrible day than to be unprepared when you need sheltering.

The first battered women's shelter in western civilization was opened in London during 1971; there were 200 shelters in the United States in 1978; and there were approximately 1,150 shelters in 1985. Many women still do not have a shelter within 50 miles of their homes. Forty-three percent of the women researched were sheltered by their families at some time, 32 percent were sheltered by friends, and 13 percent went to battered women's shelters. The proportion using battered women's shelters would have been far greater if more shelters were available.

Look in the yellow pages of your phone book, the same as you would to find a counselor or a women's group. Another way to find your closest shelter is to call the local crisis line and ask for the shelter's phone number. The counselor on the crisis line won't give you the shelter's address. Addresses are known only to shelter workers and shelter residents. That is one way of avoiding problems with enraged husbands. They can call on the phone, but they can't visit. The federal government has published a shelter directory, as have a number of states. These directories should be available in your local public library. Finally, any social service/counseling agency or women's center will be able to refer you to the nearest shelter.

In addition, some cities are developing safe houses to supplement shelters. A safe house is a private residence in which battered women are welcome. Like battered women's shelters, the addresses of safe houses are kept secret. Safe houses are generally smaller than shelters, and may have room for only one or two battered women and their children at one time.

## What Can You Expect?

Shelters provide simple accommodations for a small number of battered women and their children. You can expect to share housekeeping tasks and cooking facilities. The people who run the shelter care about battered women. They will talk with you about your situation and help you to make plans for your future. Most shelters have a social worker or other professional counselor available during the day, although you will spend most of your time talking with other battered women and with paraprofessional staff members who do not have advanced degrees in counseling. These staff members have usually overcome their own victimization at some time in the past. Working with hundreds of battered women over the years, they have developed real expertise. If you need help from professionals, these shelter workers will refer you to lawyers, physicians or other professionals who are sympathetic to battered women.

When you go to a shelter, the choice of when to leave is entirely your own. Shelter workers will respect your freedom to return to your husband, to deal with him in any way you wish, or to begin a new life. Should you opt for a new life, they will help you to make living arrangements. The need for shelter space is so great that most shelters must limit your stay in order to serve as many women as possible. Even worse, the shelter may be so full that you will be placed on a waiting list. In the meantime, you may be able to participate in one of the women's groups sponsored by the shelter. Some shelters have made arrangements with a local motel or hotel and can send you there if you have an emergency while they are filled to capacity.

You can expect to make friends with both staff members and other battered women during your stay at a shelter. Continuing some of these relations, after you have returned home or set up a new household for yourself, serves as an informal follow-up. The formal part of the follow-up occurs if you participate regularly in one of the women's groups sponsored by the shelter. Also, you can work out other ways of keeping in touch with shelter staff, such as through regular phone calls.

## Shelters Are Effective

The 854 women who completed questionnaires reported seeking shelter on over 3,000 occasions, an average of more than three times per woman. Family, friends and battered women's shelters were the main sources of sheltering. Battered women's shelters received very high effectiveness ratings from the women, 44 percent of whom gave shelters the highest possible rating. The following comments from the women's letters reveal why they hold shelters in high regard.

I and my one month old son got away from my husband six months ago, and went to a women's crisis center where I learned a lot and received much help.

I finally called the shelter and I spoke to a wonderful lady who told me she would call a cab which would take me to the police station where she would meet me. She was going off duty but made sure I got settled. Staying overnight at the shelter was a wonderful experience. The counselor was very helpful and she made me realize I wasn't the crazy one. I met two nice girls (sic) and the stay helped me a great deal. If I was able to work from their location I would have stayed longer. As it turned out, a lady drove me to my home with a police escort and I gathered what I could and then later my cousin picked me up and drove me to my parents' home. I truly didn't want to involve them but I didn't have much of a choice.

Through a shelter for abused and battered women, I got my foothold on a new future. A new start.

Today I am furthering my education, have an apartment of my own and I work full time at the shelter I fled to when I needed help. I thank God there were people there who cared... One year ago I found out there was a shelter for abused women. I had been beaten the night I heard about the shelter. When I got off work the next morning I took my first chance for safety. I traveled fifty miles to reach the shelter and I have not returned once but to get my belongings.

Battered women's shelters offer a combination of services that cannot be found in any other type of helping organization. Shelter services to battered wives include separation from the batterer, protection from outside influences, and security from the possibility that the batterer will force his way into the shelter. Most battered women have not experienced this degree of personal safety and the opportunity to freely plan their futures since early in their marriages. It is not just a matter of physical protection. Wife-beating combines physical assaults with sustained psychological abuse to produce a kind of brainwashing. Physical and psychological abuse undermine a woman's self-respect, her ability to have a balanced perspective on what is happening, and her capability for planning how to become free from the violence. Separation, protection and security are important because they temporarily break the cycle of violence, enabling battered wives to regain a balanced perspective on their lives and begin planning for the future.

Another reason for the success of battered women's shelters is the life style in the shelter, not unlike living in a unique commune. The battered women live with each other 24 hours a day, in and out of counseling sessions. By constantly exchanging experiences they learn what violent men do to their wives and also about what sometimes works in stopping the violence. Wife-battering, like other forms of brainwashing, operates by isolating the victims from the rest of society. Sheltering strikes at the heart of the batterer's isolation strategy by bringing women together. When you learn that you are not alone, that your problems are actually quite similar to the problems of other shelter clients, and that your situation is not hopeless, you are well on the way to a violence-free life.

Two final reasons for the success of battered women's shelters are the staff and the kind of help they offer abused wives. Shelter staff are as likely to be hired for their commitment to helping battered women as for their professional degrees or experience. Many have had personal experiences with wife-beating. Once victims, these women have gone on to live reasonably happy, productive and successful lives. All provide role models for shelter clients. Most battered women entering a shelter have never met a woman who successfully ended the violence in her life. Becoming acquainted with staff members who know from their own experiences that battering can be beaten is a great way to start moving toward a violence-free life yourself.

## The Future of Shelters

In our culture, perhaps as many as one-quarter of the wives will need sheltering at some time in their lives. Our research showed that the number of battered women's shelters in the United States must be multiplied by fifteen to meet the sheltering needs of abused wives. Given this level of need for sheltering by battered wives, the demonstrated effectiveness and relatively low expense of shelters, it is appropriate that we set a goal of tripling the number of battered women's shelters by 1990. Having three times as many shelters in operation as we do now still won't meet the sheltering needs of all battered women. Further expansion may be necessary if studies conducted in the late 1980's continue to find, as I have, insufficient number of shelters for the battered women.

# 9

# What Happens To The Children?

In our research, seven out of every ten battered mothers reported that their husbands assaulted their children, too. There were undoubtedly many instances of child abuse which the mothers were unaware of. The true extent to which child abuse accompanied wife abuse in the sample was probably even higher. Many children became victims when they tried to protect their mothers from their fathers' violence. Others were used as pawns in family conflicts. This chapter provides answers to basic questions you may have about what happens to children in violent families and what you can do to help them.

## The Consequences

Children who live with family violence are exposed to two dangers. The first is common among children who have been victimized themselves, and the second involves children who observe their mothers being assaulted by their fathers. Abused children who also see their mothers being mistreated are doubly disadvantaged.

The most obvious consequence of child abuse is physical injury. Yet psychological damage is probably much more extensive than physical damage, including cases of sexual abuse. Abused children may feel worthless, powerless, abandoned, rejected, guilty, depressed, anxious, or extremely hostile. These psychological pressures commonly produce psychosomatic illnesses such as headaches and upset stomachs, as well as other psychological symptoms such as severe nightmares and eating problems. Lacking a stable and supportive family life, children may become withdrawn or substitute unhealthy peer influences for family influences. Juvenile delinquency, including running away from home, is common among abused children. So are problems at school. Sexual abuse has extremely destructive effects on children, and has been linked to drug addiction, alcoholism, and prostitution in young women. Besides these problems, abused children may reject their mothers because they were unable to protect them from their fathers. Whether they reject their fathers for their cruelty or identify with them in an attempt to gain self-respect, these youngsters have been given an unbalanced view of the world.

If children are lucky enough to avoid abuse themselves, but are exposed to scenes of their mother's victimization, different negative consequences arise. Boys learn to abuse women by watching their fathers abuse their mothers. Girls begin to devalue their own feminity. What girl wants to be like a mother who is despised and beaten by her father? Girls and boys together learn that the way to settle problems is through violence and threats of violence rather than by working things out — that might invariably makes right. You may lose control over all your children if they conclude that their father won't back you up on anything you say to them.

This is only the beginning of the list of negative consequences that may occur when children see their mother abused. If the abuse is regular or the tension is generally high, they may develop the same kinds of psychosomatic illnesses and psychological symptoms as they would if beaten themselves. Realizing that their family is not like their friends' families, they may fear to bring friends home and ultimately feel alienated from them. Children's memories hang on the good times they have with their families, particularly on vacations and holidays. When violence and severe stress consistently spoil these events, they have robbed the young people of part of their childhoods.

In Chapter 6, I said that many of the counseling needs of battered women can be met by counselors without extensive clinical training. This is not the case with the abused children, or even with children who have witnessed their mothers being beaten. Children lack the adult's psychological resources and expressive ability. Someone lacking training in child psychology could easily fail to draw out your children, missing some of their most pressing concerns. My conclusion is that if you observe unusual stress symptoms or other signs of disturbances, look into the possibility of an evaluation by someone with clinical training in child psychology. A related point is that you should never postpone medical treatment for obvious or suspected physical injuries. Keeping the secret is not worth the risk of permanent physical damage.

## Moving Toward Freedom

Your efforts to end the violence may not be understood by your children. For them, things may have to get worse before they get better. As you begin to right the power imbalance in your marriage, your husband may temporarily step up his violence to try to reestablish total control of your life. This is also a time when he may attempt to turn the children against you, or to control you by openly threatening them in front of you. An increased source of stress for the children at this time is the uncertainty that your efforts introduce into the household. Consider the dislocation that occurs when you take your children to a battered women's shelter or to a friend's house. You should carefully explain as much as possible to the children, but some strategies cannot be shared for fear that one of the children will be pressured into telling your husband. For example, you may be using the threat of divorce to force your husband into therapy and have no intention of actually following through on the divorce. To your children, this could appear as if you were trying to break up the family. If you attempt to employ counterviolence against your husband, the psychological impact on your children could be devastating.

Some children seem to adjust perfectly to life in battered women's shelters. Others are overwhelmed by the experiences leading to the separation as well as conditions in the shelter. Consequently they may withdraw into themselves or misbehave. Shelters are often crowded, few have adequate play space for the children, and many lack staff who are qualified to assess the children's mental health needs. You may be preoccupied with your own affairs and it will take much self-control to meet your children's needs during this difficult period.

How will your children relate to their father and his relatives if you divorce him, seek a permanent separation, or attempt to prosecute him for his crimes against you? These questions and uncertainties produce stress. What visitation arrangement will be agreed upon? Will the children's wishes be respected? Will they still see their paternal grandparents? If they do, will the grandparents still love them? Will their father still love them? Some children may fear that they will be abused if their father is granted visitation rights. Others will be anxious about losing old friends and making new friends if moving to a new address forces them to change schools. Moving is traumatic for children who are in stable family environments; it can be far worse for children in violent marriages. Testifying in court is another traumatic event that cannot always be avoided. The effects of traumas and insecurities will vary depending on the psychological makeup of the children their age and sex.

## Talking With Your Children

You play a crucial role in the way your children react to violence, divorce, time spent in battered women's shelters, and other traumatic events. I recommend following these guidelines in talking with your children:

1. Take a strong position that your husband's behavior is wrong and damaging to you and to them.

2. Tie your actions directly to his wrong behavior. After all, you would not be taking these actions if his behavior had been acceptable.

3. Limit your condemnation to your husband's destructive behavior.

4. Reassure the children that you love them and that others who love them will continue to love them.

5. Encourage your children to express their feelings and fears so you can judge how well they are coping with the situation.

6. Be realistic about the stresses of their past life and current situation; don't whitewash everything.

7. Be positive about the future whenever possible.

Your children must understand that your husband's violence, verbal abusiveness, and any other destructive behavior is wrong. This is essential to reducing the damage their exposure to him has done to their self-images and their ideas about how family members should relate to each other. You don't want your sons to treat their future wives the way they've seen their father treat you, do you? Get counselors, friends and relatives to back you up on this. Lacking a strong position on your husband's bad behavior, you may find your children blaming you for causing the conflicts, breaking up the home, or whatever else they see going on around them.

A good principle in disciplining children is to label their behavior as undesirable, but never to refer to them as bad people. In this way, you can make society's rules clear to them without ever hurting their self-images. The same principle should be used in explaining their father's violent behavior to them. He is not bad; it is only his behavior that is unacceptable. Children identify with their parents, particularly boys with fathers and girls with mothers in their development of sex role attitudes and behavior. To say that their father is bad suggests to them that they are bad too. They have enough problems to work out without saddling them with this unnecessary baggage.

The healing power of love is no myth. It is amazing to see how much stress children can handle when they are constantly renewed through loving contacts with people who are important to them. In a loving and supportive context, it's possible to draw out their inner fears and feelings. If your children aren't talking, bring up "sensitive" subjects; ask questions and get them to explain their answers. They will appreciate your caring enough about them to spend so much time and energy getting to know them better. The information they provide will help you decide whether to seek the help of a counselor who specializes in child psychology.

The way you interpret things to your children must seem authentic. Your interpretations must strike them as accurate and consistent from one day to another. This is why it is best to be realistic about the present and the past. Your children will respect you for your honesty. The future is a different matter. To a considerable extent, you can create a positive future by communicating positive attitudes, making plans that lead to good things for you and the children, and doing your best to carry them out. Giving your children something to look forward to is important in helping them get through current difficulties. Major events such as a promised trip to a favorite relative or park are important, but don't neglect day-to-day arrangements. Make sure that your children can look forward to playtime, time with friends, and time for relaxation. Try to find positive aspects to threatening events. For example, when telling children that they are to accompany you to a shelter, mention that there may be other children there. Maybe they will make good friends at the shelter. You can never erase the suffering that children experience in a violent family. However, following the principles outlined in this chapter will enable your children to get through their present difficulties with as little pain as possible, focusing on the better things to come. Scars will remain, but remember that scars are also a sign of healing.

# 10

# What Works? Ending Marital Violence

Throughout this book, I have stressed that battered women need not passively accept their fate. The women in our study fought continuously against their husbands' abusiveness, and most of them had become free of violence before they participated in the study. They began their battle to end the violence with personal strategies they could use in the privacy of their homes: passive defense, hiding, avoidance, counterviolence, nonviolent threatening, obtaining promises from the batterer, and talking rationally about the problem. Some of these strategies were helpful, but they rarely were sufficient to permanently end the violence. As the violence continued, the women expanded their base of resources, going beyond the home to enlist the aid of both informal and formal sources of help. The informal sources of help they used were friends, family members, in-laws, and neighbors. Formal help-sources used included the police, lawyers, district attorneys, social service and counseling agencies, the clergy, doctors and nurses, and women's groups. Battered women's shelters are an important help-source. Unfortunately, there are so few shelters that most of the shelter services used by the women in the study came from family and friends instead of shelter organizations.

## What Works Best?

The last battering incident was a pivotal point in the lives of the women who were free of violence when they participated in the study. Before the final battering, their lives were pure hell; afterwards they embarked on a new and more fulfilling way of living. A crucial question is what worked best in ending the battering forever? There is no single answer to this question. The same strategies or sources of help were not the most important factors in ending the battering for every woman.

The five sources that we found most likely to work for women were: (1) lawyers, (2) women's groups, (3) battered women's shelters, (4) social service and counseling agencies, and (5) permanent separation and divorce. Factors that were found to be particularly effective were "seeking help immediately" and "raising one's own self-esteem while becoming more independent." These last two factors were not originally included in the study. However, they were spontaneously listed by many women as general advice to other battered women about how to become free of the violence.

Some women developed a combination of personal strategies and help-sources that seemed to have promise, and they consistently followed this pattern, wearing down their husbands in the process until they finally gave up beating them. Other women did not find success until they hit upon a new combination, or added a new source of help. This changed their situation at home in a matter of weeks or a few months, leaving them suddenly violence-free.

## Motivations

Why were so many husbands willing to give up their violent ways, and what gave their wives the courage to demand an end to the batterings? Our research provides us with some detailed answers to these questions. We will first look at the wives, for changes in them generally had to occur before they could put enough pressure on their husbands to be successful in ending the violent behavior.

The most commonly mentioned reason why the women were able to stand up to their husbands was that they had simply had enough. They had suffered far too long already, and decided they had to act to end the terror. This answer is deceptively simple. What it really means is that the women had grown and developed through the process of fighting the batterings. They were now strong enough to make plans to become violence-free and to act on them regardless of the consequences.

The theme of increased personal strength, self-confidence and determination was also prominent in other factors mentioned by the women:

1. Women's groups gave them confidence and information,
2. Family members gave them confidence, and
3. Social service and counseling agencies gave them confidence and aid.

Women's groups were twice as likely as family or social service agencies to be mentioned as the factor that finally gave them confidence to openly move against their husbands. The remaining factors mentioned by women were fear for self and fear for the children. Only one woman out of six cited either of these reasons as the primary source of their motivation in ending the violence.

The women we interviewed in depth saw both positive and negative motivations as responsible for their husbands' willingness to cease their violence. A few of the batterers modified their behavior because they accepted changes in their wives and were now willing to have a more equal relationship. They preferred to dominate their wives completely, but valued their marital relations so much that they were willing to let their wives have a say in things rather than lose them.

Most of the men, unfortunately, had less positive motivations for giving up their violent habits. They did so only because they feared the embarrassment and social consequences of getting a divorce, or that they would actually be arrested and imprisoned like common criminals if the batterings continued. We might say that they were forced into decent behavior against their will, and that they had to be dragged every foot of the way. *In short, it was the irresistible ultimatum rather than a progressive sensitivity to the injustice and cruelty of the batterings that ended the violence in most of the marriages studied.*

The essence of the change that must occur for wife-beating to end without the woman's total subjugation is that there must be a shift in the marital power balance. Wife-beating is primarily a tool that men use to maintain and increase their dominance. Although a few batterers are seriously mentally ill, and a somewhat larger number have a severe drinking problem, these factors are probably responsible for only a small portion of the wife-beating that occurs each day. For marital violence to end, the wife must increase her power within the marital relationship. Counseling and talks with friends and relatives help increase a wife's power by allowing her to gain personal strength and a more positive self-image. The police, lawyers, and district attorneys (and also family and friends) increase her power by coming into the marital conflict on her side. Nonviolent threats gain their effectiveness by referring to these sources of power. Our study shows that the cessation of violence is not always associated with personal growth by the husbands, but it invariably is at least partially the product of personal growth by the wives. Husbands who grow as they work out their problems usually can be led to end the violence, or spontaneously do so. If they do not grow, the prognosis is less positive. It is likely that they will only free their wives from the bonds of violence if they are forced to do so through threats and other kinds of pressure. Living with such men is less than ideal, even after the violence has ended.

## After Violence Ends

While you are being beaten, it may appear that everything would be rosy in your marriage if the violence were to end. If the marriage was a satisfying one to begin with, and if the violence has not been severe, it may be that the cessation of violence will leave you with a relatively happy marriage — one worth continuing. But what if you were originally married because of pregnancy or parental pressure, and you and your husband never were close? Or what about the possibility that your marriage has many severe problems which are obscured by the violence? If this is true, the cessation of violence may leave you with an empty feeling as fear abates without being replaced by love and mutual understanding.

Many of the women who became violence-free while still living with their husbands eventually separated and obtained a divorce. For these women, there either never was a relationship worth maintaining or the violence ate away what was satisfying in the marriage until nothing remained. In our study, the most important factor in a wife's decision to eventually divorce her husband was her satisfaction with the marriage. Having conquered fear and suffered much, these women were no longer willing to remain in marriages that offered little more than empty rituals.

## Battered Wives Speak Out

The women in our research are in a unique position, because of their experiences with overcoming violence, to offer general advice to other women who have not yet become free of violence. Listed below are the ten points that they mentioned most often in their advice to battered women:

1. Obtain a divorce, separate, see a lawyer.
2. Get counseling for self and/or the batterer.
3. Secure help immediately; don't let the pattern become established.
4. Be independent and raise your self-esteem.
5. Tell others about the violence; keep no secrets.
6. Be firm with the batterer.
7. Call the police to arrest the batterer, file charges and follow through on the prosecution.
8. Ask friends and neighbors for help.
9. Go to a battered women's shelter.
10. Go to women's groups and women's therapists.

This is not advice from professional experts who may have never been abused or who have never had to fear what the next day would bring. This is advice from women who are experts by experience, who have suffered at the hands of their husbands and lovers. Most of them are now violence-free, and are looking back at what they found to be most helpful to them in ending the violence in their lives. See what you think as you read their advice in their words.

> ...be willing to take definite and immediate steps to end the beatings. I chose to do this by obtaining a restraining order and a divorce. In my case, staying alive was worth the unpleasantness associated with divorce

[proceedings].

The best service that could be launched for battered women is a massive public education campaign.

Realize that it happens not to poor, retarded and uneducated people — but to your neighbor, your friends.

The best advice I have for other battered women is to seek counseling. I sought counseling through the local mental health clinic after which I regained self-confidence and self-esteem. Prior to counseling, I believed it was my lot in life to accept the situation.

My advice for battered women is "quit kidding yourself that the violence will stop." Seek legal counsel or a therapist who deals with battered women. The Women's Crisis Center was an excellent support system to me. And finally...SPEAK UP!

My advice to any young woman whose husband has hit her, would be to leave on the very first time and *never* give him a second chance.

Life is too short and precious to live in fear and always be afraid. Talk to a pastor or a doctor about your problem. Walk proud and don't be ashamed.

My advice is to realize that you as a person have worth. Have faith in yourself and realize there is a better life for you somewhere — *LEAVE!* Promises are nice, but they rarely come true. There are sure to be people out there who love you and will help you in your new life.

Get a job, a car and checking account of your own. Be

ready to leave at any time. Take someone into your confidence. If you cover for [the batterer], he will be secretly triumphant in "getting away" with what he's done. Don't make idle threats about leaving him — DO IT! And if your children are victims, RUN to the nearest Department of Social Services! If a man refuses to admit he has a problem and refuses to seek help, the chain of violence will never be broken. YOU must take the steps yourself to save your children and yourself.

Leave, the children will be harmed. By example the children will suffer from what they hear and see. DON'T STAY FOR THE SAKE OF THE CHILDREN.

The strong character of these women comes through in their general advice to women currently being battered. At one time, most felt weak in dealing with their husbands, but that is no longer true. Faced with a problem that seemed insurmountable, which in most cases continued for many years, they triumphed over it. In doing so, they developed an inner strength which also aided them in making other changes in their lives. This is the amazing transformation through which victims became victors, and in the process have become an inspiration to us all.

## Why Wife Abuse?

My research revealed that the more frequently a man socialized with his friends, the more severely and extensively he battered his wife. This finding, when integrated with existing knowledge about the relationships among masculinity, subcultures, and violence, lead me to propose a new understanding of wife-beating.

According to my theory, battering husbands have developed standards of gratification which demand that they dominate their wives and children. When this domination is threatened, they feel deprived, suffer mental distress, and react with a rage that appears to be uncontrollable, but is actually contrived to reestablish the domination patterns that meet their standards of gratification. Men are not born with any particular standards of gratification. Their standards are learned through their experiences in our society, and they vary in strength directly with the support the standards receive from their friends and family members.

Many batterers begin to develop standards of gratification demanding domestic dominance when they see their mothers dominated by their fathers and experience this domination themselves as children. The idea that masculinity requires domination is further supported by many of our society's patriarchal, sexist ideas and social arrangements. These patriarchal ideas and social arrangements are survivals from a time when women were even more extensively oppressed — forbidden to vote, largely excluded from higher education, and practically held as captive in their own homes.

Standards of gratification developed during childhood can persist throughout life with the assistance of general cultural support for male dominance. But the fullest development of standards for gratification through dominance that lead to marital violence occurs in those men who are heavily immersed in social relationships with male friends who constantly reinforce these standards. There is no national lobby favoring wife-beating. However, the many male friends and acquaintances who support the patriarchal dominance of the family and the use of violence to enforce it may amount to what we might call a masculine culture of violence.

This is not a culture that is confined to a single social class, religion, occupational grouping, or race. It is spread throughout all parts of society. Men are influenced by their friends to accept common definitions of the situation, norms, values, and the beliefs about male dominance and the necessity of keeping their wives "in line." These violence-supporting social relations may occur at any time and in any place. For most wife-beaters they probably center around work, involvement in informal participatory sports activities, and socializing in certain bars and similar social gathering places from which women are largely excluded. Even in mixed-sex parties, men sometimes form all-male groups from which women are excluded by a variety of subtle social pressures so that "man talk" can occur uncensored by the presence of women. Pornography — both hard core porn and "girlie magazines" — is an important source of communication for the masculine culture which supports violence and demeans womanhood. Because our study did not directly deal with the idea of a male culture of violence, we can only guess at its broad outlines. To learn more about this culture of violence we must carry out extensive research on battering males.

Wife-beating is a form of oppression which, in its extreme manifestations, takes on the character of brainwashing. The victim is so totally dominated and degraded, and her self-esteem is lowered so far, that she comes to exemplify what Lenore Walker, in her books *The Battered Woman* and *The Battered Woman Syndrome,* has referred to as "learned helplessness." By being nice to his wife after battering her, many wife-beaters are able to form what is called a traumatic bond between them.

> [My husband] says he loves me, and everytime I would take the boys and leave or file for divorce he'd cry and promise me the moon. Within a week, things would start over as before.
>
> I left numerous times before I was actually strong enough to hold out against all the "sweet" talk and promises.

After he pushes, hits or throws something at me he's usually sorry within the hour...

The traumatic bond takes the place of the love, understanding and mutual support that holds healthy marriages together. The battered wife in these families forms a common bond with her oppressor in much the same way as the victims in Nazi concentration camps sometimes identified with their guards and as hostages sometimes identify with their captors.

This process was first described by Anna Freud as identification with the aggressor. According to Freud, this process leads the victim to accept the aggressors' definitions of themselves, producing self-hatred or a redirected aggression toward others who are defined as similar to the self. In violent families, this redirected aggression can become child abuse. A battering husband probably beats the children, too. What's worse, his mistreatment probably increases the chances that his wife will abuse her children. Freud said two things were necessary to produce identification with the aggressor: an extreme power imbalance between aggressor and victim, and occasional punitive behavior from the aggressor to the victim. These conditions are met perfectly in severe cases of wife-beating. They may also be met where initial conditioning with violence has so sensitized the victim that it is only necessary for the aggressor to scream, shout, and pound the table in order to dominate his family.

Dutton and Painter draw on studies of animals and infants as well as of adults in a variety of powerless, violent situations to show that traumatic bonding and the cycle of violence is more a universal law of behavior than something unusual which happens only to battered wives. In their words, "When the physical punishment is administered at intermittent intervals, and when it is interspersed with permissive and friendly contact, the phenomenon of 'traumatic bonding' seems most powerful" (1981: p. 149). This cycle effect is no doubt strongest when the wife's marital satisfaction, apart from the batterings, is relatively high, when she still loves her husband, and when his behavior after the batterings is particularly apologetic and pleasant. As I understand it, wife-beating is most related to the husband's background, not the wife's. It is his insatiable demand for dominance, based on standards of dominance that are unrealistically high and an affront to human dignity, that is the driving engine of his violence. He may be supported in his abusive behavior and his degradation of women by some of his male friends, his reading of pornography, and other contacts with what I call the male culture of violence. He uses both violence and psychological abuse to keep you subservient to his wishes, combining them into a form of brainwashing that saps your self-confidence.

This is a bleak picture. Some men are willing to change. Others must be abandoned. My research shows that battered women can become violence-free if they find the combination of personal strategies, informal and formal help-sources that is right for them. If you or someone you know is being battered, I hope that the experiences of the one thousand abused women summarized in this book will help you become free of violence too.

# 11

# Summary of Recommendations

This final chapter contains recommendations drawn from the entire book so readers can have them available in one place for quick reference. It concludes with six recommendations for social change that have developed out of my research.

## Three Rules For Using Personal Strategies

- Nothing works unless you convince your husband that you are dead serious about ending the batterings.

- Verbal strategies based on caring are not worth trying unless your husband cares a great deal about you.

- Don't allow a pattern of violence to develop in your marriage.

## Evaluating Your Marriage

The more "yes" answers you can give to the following questions, the worse your marriage.

- Does your husband try to undermine your self-confidence every time he gets a chance?

- Does he force sex on you against your will? If he does, you should consider this rape.
- Does he sometimes beat your children too?
- Does he show any pleasure in your suffering?
- Does he have friends who support his beating you, or who beat their wives?
- Has he ever beaten you while you were pregnant?
- Have you ever been beaten so badly that you had to go to the doctor or hospital?
- Are you afraid that he might assault friends or relatives if they were to help you hide out after a beating?
- Do you believe that he might seriously or permanently injure you or the children at some time in the future?
- Do you believe that he is committed to violence as a way of solving his problem, and of controlling you?
- Has his violence against you continued for a long time?
- Does your husband beat you every time you try to have some life of your own apart from his domination (for example, having a close friend, taking a night class, or being in a bowling league)?

## Principles For Talking With Your Children

- Take a strong position that your husband's behavior is

wrong and damaging to you and to them.

- Relate your actions directly to his wrong behavior.

- Try to limit your condemnation of your husband's behavior to his violence and avoid making global judgments about him.

- Reassure the children that you love them and that others who love them now will continue to love them in the future.

- Draw them out about their feelings and fears so you can judge how well they are coping with the situation.

- Be realistic about the stresses of their past life and current situation.

- Be positive about the future whenever possible.

## What Works Best?

- Women's groups.

- Battered women's shelters.

- Lawyers.

- Social service and counseling agencies.

- Permanent separation or divorce.

- Seeking help immediately.

110   ENDING THE VIOLENCE

- Raising one's self-esteem while becoming more independent.

## Advice To Battered Women

Because of their experiences with violence, the 1,000 women I studied are in a unique position to offer general advice to other women who are being battered. These are the ten points that they mentioned most often in their advice to those who are still battered.

- Obtain a divorce, separate, see a lawyer.
- Get counseling for self and/or the batterer.
- Secure help immediately; don't let the pattern become established.
- Be independent and raise your self-esteem.
- Tell others about the violence; keep no secrets.
- Be firm with the batterer.
- Call the police to arrest the batterer, file charges and follow through on the prosecution.
- Ask friends and neighbors for help.
- Go to a battered women's shelter.
- Go to women's groups and women's therapists.

## Recommendations For Social Change

These recommendations are included for those who wish to know about the social changes that will be required to substantially reduce the problem of wife-beating in western civilization.

1. *Battered women need to receive advice about the wealth of personal strategies and community resources that they can use in ending their victimization.* Information should be provided through all possible avenues, including the media, social service agencies, battered women's organizations, and lawyers' offices. In addition, this information should be made available in places such as supermarkets, welfare offices, and shopping malls. Making information about wife-beating readily available will help women prepare to defend themselves, keeping the pattern of abuse from becoming established in their families. There is also a need to continually re-evaluate and refine the data on personal strategies and help-sources.

2. *The heavy use of sheltering by the battered women in the study implies that the need for sheltering services is even greater than has previously been estimated by the supporters of battered women's shelters. Additional public funds should be diverted to open new battered women's shelters.* In addition, there should be a guarantee of continuing, full support for existing shelters. It is clear that there will never be enough shelters to meet the needs of the battered women, even if many new facilities are opened. Each state, country and municipality should consider the possibility of providing financial support for private citizens who are giving shelter to battered women and their children through informal helping networks. This is the only way to meet the needs of those battered women who fall beyond the capacities of existing and future shelter organizations. The technical problems involved in such a reimbursement program would be considerable, but they are not beyond the realm of possibility. Pam-

phlets intended to help battered women deal with their husbands can also be designed for use by members of informal helping resource networks offering support.

3. *The very high effectiveness ratings given by the battered wives to women's groups suggests that it would be efficient to use agency and general public funds to support them.* They can often be efficiently combined with shelter services under multipurpose umbrella agencies. Where additional women's groups are developed within existing agencies, they should be allowed to exist independently of the bureaucratic structure of the agency and its treatment modality preferences as much as possible. Our findings tell us that the once-battered wives who are typically responsible for the operation of these groups are remarkably capable of delivering effective services to battered wives. Rather than weakening these services by making them conform to traditional service delivery models, existing agencies should look carefully at the treatment models used by women's groups to determine what elements of these models can be incorporated into their own service delivery systems.

4. *With the exception of women's groups, a significant proportion of all of the individuals in helping agencies and criminal justice organizations need training in the nature of family violence, the needs of battered women, and the personal strategies and community resources that are effective in combatting marital violence.* The use of once-battered wives as staff members should be encouraged.

5. *The dismal ratings of help received from police departments suggests that their services to battered women should be targeted by public interest groups for immediate upgrading.* Police officers should receive additional training in the handling of domestic disputes within the framework of the law. In addition, they should also distribute folders referring them to other appropriate help-sources.

6. *If violent husbands are heavily enmeshed in a peer subculture that supports their violence they must change their friends to sustain any gain made in treatment.* I believe that self-help groups built on the model of Alcoholics Anonymous will be the most successful in changing the behavior of wife batterers. Batterers who do not have support from a male peer subculture of violence will be less resistent to individual therapy, marital therapy, and standard group therapy techniques.

## Appendix
# For Further Reading

All of these items should be available in your local library or through an interlibrary loan.

Bochnak, Elizabeth. *Women's Self-Defense Cases: Theory and Practice.* Charlottesville, Va.: Michie, 1981.

Bowker, Lee H. *Beating Wife-Beating.* Lexington, Mass.: D. C. Heath, 1983.

Bowker, Lee, H. *Masculinities and Violence.* Thousand Oaks, Calif.: Sage 1998.

Boylan, Ann M., and Nadine Taub. *Adult Domestic Violence: Constitutional, Legislative and Equitable Issues.* Washington D.C.: Legal Service Corp., Research Institute, 1981.

Browne, Angela, *When Battered Women Kill.* New York: Free Press, 1987.

Counts, D. A., J. K. Brown, and J. C. Campbell (eds.). *Sanctions and Sanctuary: Cultural Perspectives on the Beating of Wives.* Boulder, Co.: Westview, 1992.

Dobash, R. E. and R. P. Dobash. *Violence Against Wives: A Case Against the Patriarchy.* New York: Free Press, 1979.

Dobash, R. E. and R. P. *Women, Violence, and Social Change.* London: Routledge, 1992.

Dutton, Don G. *The Domestic Assault of Women.* Boston: Allyn and Bacon, 1988.

Dutton, Mary Ann. *Empowering and Healing the Battered Woman: A Model for Assessment and Intervention.* New York: Springer, 1992.

Gelles, Richard J., and Donileen R. Loseke (eds.). *Current Controversies on Family Violence.* Thousand Oaks, Calif.: Sage, 1993.

Gelles, Richard J., and Murray A. Straus. *Intimate Violence: The Causes and Consequences of Abuse in the American Family.* New York: Simon and Schuster, 1988.

Giles-Sims, Jean. *Wife Battering: A Systems Theory Approach.* New York, Guilford Press, 1983.

Gondolf, Edward W., and E. R. Fisher. *Battered Women as Survivors: An Alternative to Treating Learned Helplessness.* New York: Lexington, 1988.

Gordon, Linda. *Heroes of Their Own Lives: The Politics and History of Family Violence.* New York: Penguin, 1988.

Herman, Judith. *Trauma and Recovery: The Aftermath of Violence — From Domestic Abuse to Political Terror.* New York: Basic Books, 1992.

Jones, Ann. *Next Time She'll Be Dead:Battering and How to Stop It.* Boston: Bacon, 1994.

Kirkwood, C. *Leaving Abusive Partners.* Thousand Oaks, Calif.: Sage, 1993.

Koss, Mary P. et al. *No Safe Haven: Male Violence Against Women at Home, at Work, and in the Community.* Washington D.C.: American Psychological Association, 1994.

NiCarthy, Ginny, Getting Free: A Handbook for Women in Abusive Relationships, Seattle, WA: Seal Press, 1982.

Pagelow, Mildred D. *Woman Battering: Victims and Their Experiences.* Beverly Hills, Calif.: Sage, 1981.

Pagelow, Mildren D. *Family Violence.* New York: Praeger, 1984.

Pence, E., and M. Paymar. *Education Groups for Men Who Batter: The Duluth Model.* New York: Springer, 1993.

Renzetti, Claire. *Violent Betrayal: Partner Abuse in Lesbian Relationships.* Thousand Oaks, Calif.: Sage, 1992.

Rodgers, K. *Wife Assault in Canada.* Ottawa: Ministry of Supply and Services, 1994.

Russell, Diana E. *Rape in Marriage.* New York: Macmillan, 1982.

Straus, Murray A., and Richard J. Gelles. *Physical Violence in American Families: Risk Factors and Adaptations to Violence in 8,145 Families.* New Brunswick, N.J.: Transaction, 1990.

Straus, Murray A., Richard Gelles, and Suzanne Steinmetz. *Behind Closed Doors: Violence in the American Family.* Garden City, N.Y.: Doubleday, 1980.

Tifft, Larry L. *Battering of Women: The Failure of Intervention and the Case for Prevention.* Boulder Co.: Westview, 1993.

Walker, Lenore E. *The Battered Woman Syndrome.* New York: Springer, 1984.

Walker, Lenore. *Terrifying Love: Why Battered Women Kill and How Society Responds.* New York: HarperCollins, 1989.

Yllo, Kersti and Michele Bograd (eds.). *Feminist Perspectives on Wife Abuse.* Thousand Oaks, Calif.: Sage, 1988.

## Technical Reports on the Author's Research on Battered Women

Bowker, Lee H. "Battered Women and the Clergy: An Evaluation," *Journal of Pastoral Care,* 36 (1982): 226-34.

Bowker, Lee H., "Police Services to Battered Women: Bad or Not So Bad?" *Criminal Justice and Behavior,* 9 (1982): 476-94.

Bowker, Lee H. "Battered Wives, Lawyers and District Attorneys: An Examination of Law in Action," *Journal of Criminal Justice,* 2 (1983): 403-12.

Bowker, Lee H. "Marital Rape: A Distinct Syndrome?" *Social Casework,* 64 (1983): 348-52.

Bowker, Lee H. *Beating Wife-Beating.* Lexington, Mass.: D.C. Heath, 1983.

Bowker, Lee H. "Coping With Wife Abuse: Personal and Social Networks," in Albert R. Roberts, *Battered Women and Their Families.* New York: Springer Publishing Co., (1984): 168-191.

Bowker, Lee H. "Battered Wives and the Police: A National Study of Usage and Effectiveness," *Police Studies,* 7 (1984): 84-93.

Donato, Katherine and Lee H. Bowker. "Understanding the Helpseeking Behavior of Battered Women: A Comparison of Traditional Service Agencies and Women's Groups," *International Journal of Women's Studies,* 7 (1984): 99-109.

Bowker, Lee, H. "The Effects of National Development on the Position of Married Women in the Third World: The Case of Wife Beating," *International Journal of Comparative and Applied Criminal Justice,* 9 (1985):1-13.

Bowker, Lee H., and Lorie Maurer. "The Effectiveness of Counseling Services Utilized by Battered Women," *Women and Therapy,* 5 (1986): 65-82.

Bowker, Lee H., "The Meaning of Wife-Beating," *Currents: Issues in Education and Human Development,* 4 (1986): 37-43.

Bowker, Lee H., and Lorie Maurer, "The Medical Treatment of Battered Wives," *Women and Health,* 12 (1987): 25-45.

Bowker, Lee H. "Battered Women as Consumers of Legal Services: Reports from a National Survey," *Response to the Victimization of Women and Children,* 10 (1987): 10-17.

Bowker, Lee H., Michelle Arbitell, and J. Richard McFerron. "On the Relationship Between Wife Abuse and Child Abuse," in *Feminist Perspectives on Wife Abuse,* Kersti Yllo and Michele Bograd (eds.). Beverly Hills, Calif.: Sage Publications, (1988): 158-74.

Bowker, Lee H. "Religious Victims and Their Religious Leaders: Services Delivered to One Thousand Battered Women by the Clergy," in *Abuse and Religion: When Praying Isn't Enough,* Anne L. Horton and Judith Ann Williamson (eds.). Lexington, Mass.: D.C. Heath, (1988): 229-34.

Bowker, Lee H., "Considering Marriage: Avoiding Marital Violence," *Family Life Educator,* 6 (1987-88): 4-9. (Reprinted as a pamphlet by ETR Associates' National Family Life Network. Now available in a second edition.)

Bowker, Lee H., "The Effect of Methodology on Subjective Estimates of the Differential Effectiveness of Personal Strategies and Help-Sources Used by Battered Women," in *Coping with Family Violence: Research and Policy Perspectives,* Gerald T. Hotaling, David Finkelhor, John T. Kirkpatrick and Murray Straus (eds.). Beverly Hills, Calif.: Sage Publications, 1988, pp. 80-92.

Brendtro, Mary and Lee H. Bowker. "Battered Women: How Can Nurses Help?" *Issues in Mental Health Nursing,* 10 (1989):169-180.

Bowker, Lee H., "A Battered Woman's Problems are Social, Not Psychological," in *Current Controversies on Family Violence,* Richard J. Gelles and Donileen R. Loseke (eds.). Beverly Hills, Calif.: Sage, (1993): 154-65.

Bowker, Lee H. "Existing Community-Based Alternatives Will Not Deter Serious Woman Batterers," *Sociological Imagination,* 31 (1994): 50-62.

Bowker, Lee H. "Reply to Salem's Crime, Public Policy and Woman Battering," *Sociological Imagination,* 32 (1995): 205-10.

Bowker, Lee H., "The Sociologists, Gangs, and Battered Women: Representing the Discipline in the Courts," in *Witnessing for Sociology: Sociologists in Court,* Pamela J. Jenkins and J. Stephen Kroll-Smith, (eds.). Westport, Conn.: Greenwood Publishing Group, (1996): 149-63.

Bowker, Lee H., "Masculinities and Violence," Thousand Oaks, Calif.: Sage, 1998.

# INDEX

Adler, Emily S., 114.
Age, 5, 31.
Alcohol abuse, 3, 8, 15, 20, 21, 27, 51, 55, 98.
Armed forces, 5, 9.
Australian Institute of Criminology, 1.
Avoidance, 19, 26, 27, 30-32.
Back, Susan M., 114.
Barnett, Ellen R., 114.
Battered women's shelters, 33, 42, 43, 47, 49, 51, 53, 65, 66, 71, 79, 81-87, 91, 96, 100, 111, 112.
Batterers, characteristics of, 5, 6.
Batterings, characteristics of, 8-14.
Blaming, of victims, 14, 15.
Bochnak, Elizabeth, 114.
Boylan, Ann M., 114.
Canadian Advisory Council on the Status of Women, 1.
Case history, 2-5.
Center for Women Policy Studies, 114.
Cessation, of battering, 95-102, 109, 110; See also Effectiveness.
Child abuse, 8, 12-14, 29, 30, 37, 50, 53, 54, 88, 89, 101, 102, 105.
Children, of batterers and their wives, 6, 88-94, 108, 109; See also Child abuse.
Class, socioeconomic, 5, 31, 80, 101, 103.
Clergy, 40, 51, 66, 70-73, 78, 80, 101.
Counseling, professional, 4, 18, 24, 33, 40, 44, 46-49, 51, 53, 56, 66-75, 78, 79, 83, 85, 90, 93, 96, 100, 101, 112.
Counterviolence, 19, 28-31, 91.
Cycle of violence, 22, 105, 106.
Disagreements, marital, 6; See also Dominance, by batterers.
District attorneys, 24, 40, 53, 55-58, 60-65, 98.
Divorce, 4, 5, 21-24, 32, 38, 53, 55, 70, 71, 91, 96, 99, 100.

Dobash, R.E., 1, 114.
Dobash, R.P., 1, 114.
Dominance, by batterers, 2-7, 16, 20, 24, 27, 32, 43, 44, 46, 54, 74, 97, 98, 103-106.
Donato, Katherine, 119.
Dutton, Don, 105, 115.
Education, 5, 80.
Effectiveness, of battered women's shelters, 84-87, 91, 96, 112; of clergy, 71, 72, 78; of counselors, 68, 73, 74, 78, 96, 97; of district attorneys, 61-63, 65, 98; of informal help-sources, 44-45, 97; of lawyers, 61-63, 65, 96, 98; of personal strategies, 30, 31; of physicians and nurses, 49; of police, 57, 60-63, 65, 98, 112; of women's groups, 77, 78, 80, 81, 96, 97.
Families, help from, 33-39, 53, 56, 59, 84, 93, 97, 106.
Families, violent, char. of, 6.
Finkelhor, David, 115.
Fleming, Jennifer B., 115.
Freud, Anna, 105, 115.
Friends, help from, 3, 27, 33-35, 37, 39-41, 53, 54, 89, 93, 100, 106.
Gelles, Richard J., 115, 117.
Giles-Sims, Jean, 115.
Hiding, 19, 24, 25, 31.
Home ownership, 6.
Hotaling, Gerald T., 115.
Incest, 13, 14, 88, 89.
In-laws, help from, 38, 39, 45.
Jealousy, 7, 16, 27.
Landis, Leslie, 114.
Lawyers, help from 4, 10, 24, 36, 39, 40, 43, 45, 48, 49, 51-53, 55, 60-65, 84, 96, 98, 101, 111.
Learned helplessness, 104.
Male culture of violence, 9, 18, 26, 28, 64, 103-106, 113.
Marriages, evaluation of, 53-55, 107, 108.

Massachusetts Coalition of Battered Women Service Groups, 115.
Maurer, Lorie, 118, 119.
Mental illness, of batterers, 14, 15, 18.
Miscarriages, from batterings, 8, 11, 12.
Money, control of, by batterers, 17, 25.
Moore, Donna, 115.
Neighbors, help from, 41, 42, 56, 100.
NiCarthy, Ginny, 115.
Nurses, 48, 49.
Pagelow, Mildred D., 115, 116.
Painter, Susan Lee, 105, 115.
Parents, of batterer and wife, violence between, 7, 15, 31.
Passive defense, 19, 25, 26, 31.
Personal strategies, 19-33, 96, 106, 107, 112.
Physicians, 48-51, 54, 84.
Police, 23, 24, 41, 42, 44, 55-65, 98, 100, 112.
Pornography, 16, 104, 106.
Pregnant, battered while, 3, 8, 11, 59.
Premarital violence, 2, 3, 7, 8.
Promising, 19, 21, 22, 30, 31, 44, 62.
Psychological abuse, 3, 8, 10, 16-18, 46, 53, 86, 104-106.
Race, 5, 80, 103.
Rape, marital, 3, 8, 11, 13, 53.
Religion, 5, 103; *See also* Clergy.
*Response to Violence in the Family and Sexual Abuse*, 116.
Restraining orders, 45, 52.
Roberts, Albert R., 116, 118.
Roy, Maria, 116.
Russell, Diana E., 116.
Safe houses, 83.
Sample, description of, 5, 6.
Satisfaction, marital, 6, 99.

Scott, Jocelynne, 1.
Self-confidence, of battered wives, 32, 40, 43, 46, 47, 53, 69, 70, 76, 77, 86, 96, 97, 100-102, 106.
Separation, marital, 6, 21, 33, 36, 38, 40, 42, 43, 53, 71, 72, 96, 101; *See also* Divorce.
Sex, forced, *See* Rape, marital.
Sheltering, with friends and family, 3, 27, 38-45; with formal organizations, *See* Battered women's shelters.
Social service agency, *See* Counseling, professional.
Solicitor General Canada, 1.
Sports, violent, 6, 16.
Standards of gratification, 103.
Steinmetz, Suzanne K., 116, 117.
Straus, Murray, 1, 115-117.
Talking, with the batterer, 19-21, 30, 31; with the children, 92, 93, 108, 109.
Taub, Nadine, 114.
Threatening, nonviolent, 19, 23, 24, 30, 31-33, 52, 98.
Theories, of wife-beating, 14-18, 102-106.
Torture, of battered wives, 11, 13, 26, 53.
Traumatic bond, 104, 105.
United States Commission on Civil Rights, 117.
University of Regina, 1.
Verbal abuse, *See* Psychological abuse.
Walker, Lenore, 104, 117.
Weapons, assault with, 8, 10, 11, 28, 29, 37, 40, 59, 61.
Wives, battered, characteristics of, 5, 6.
Women's groups, 33, 40, 47, 49, 51, 65-67, 71, 75-81, 84, 96, 97, 100, 101, 112.